Lost Shangri La

(Glimpses of Ancient Kashmir)

" If you want to destroy a nation,
then destroy its history and heritage"

— *A Tartar Proverb*

Lost Shangri La
(Glimpses of Ancient Kashmir)

by
S. Sapru

Foreword by
M.V. Kamath

Decent Books
New Delhi

Published and printed by:
Decent Books
D-36/A-1, Mohan Garden
Najafgarh Road
New Delhi - 110 059

Distributed by:
D.K. Printworld (P) Ltd.
Regd. office : '*Sri Kunj*', F-52, Bali Nagar
New Delhi - 110 015
Phones : (011) 545-3975, 546-6019; *Fax* : (011) 546-5926
E-mail: dkprint@4mis.com

ISBN 81-86921-17-6

First Published in India in 2001

Foreword

FOR a long time now the State of Jammu and Kashmir has been in the news largely because of terrorism and killings. Not a day passes without reports of murder and mayhem in the newspapers. There are no two opinions as to who the terrorists are and what specifically they are after. Their aim is to detach the State from India and incorporate it into Pakistan on the grounds that Kashmir is a Muslim-majority State that should, in the nature of things, be part of Islamic Pakistan. The argument that India has more Muslims that Pakistan and by that criterion Kashmir's fate should ever be linked with that of India makes no dent on the thinking in Islamabad. Nor is that fact that Kashmir was not always Muslim, conceded by Pakistani leaders. Islam was brutally imposed on Kashmir only towards the middle of the fourteenth century. Till then the people of Kashmir were Hindus. As we know from Kalhana's *Rajatarangini*, the original inhabitants of Kashmir were Shaivite Hindus though, in later years it was also to become the fountain-head of Mahayana Buddhism. Kalhana in his work mentions the existence of the four-fold *varnas* but following large-scale conversions *circa* AD 1320 only the Brahmans remained. They subsequently came to be known as *pandits*, a description that has come down to this day.

Who are the *pandits*? What are their antecedents? Even more importantly, what has been their contribution to the culture and ethos of their beautiful land? One of the earliest and authoritative works on Kashmir is that of P.N.K. Bamzai, but in this work, *Lost Shangri La*, S. Sapru brings to us the beauty and greatness of this fabulous land in all its splendour. As Sapru so rightly notes, Kashmir is the symbol of the cultural unity of India.

In ancient times, Kashmir was known as a centre of learning.

Here grew the arts of music, dance, sculpture and language. For upward of two thousand years, Kashmir had been the home of Sanskrit learning. From this small but fertile valley, issued masterpieces of history, poetry, fable, romance and philosophy. Scholars from all over India and even from distant China flocked to Kashmir to imbibe learning. Sapru recounts in meaningful detail the literary and artistic achievements of Kashmiris like Jayaditta and Vamana, Bhatta and Jagadhara, not to mention Pingala and Kshemendra. Abhinavagupta wrote profusely on aesthetics and his later work was completed by his disciple Allata Kavyaprakasha.

The point to Sapru's work is that there is more to Kashmir than that present-day spate of mindless violence. If, towards the end, he makes a detour to write about mythology, it is to stress Kashmir's links with the rest of India, stretching, as it is often said from Kashmir to Kanyakumari. So many are the feasts and festivities observed in Kashmir that are common to all India that Pakistan's bogus claims to Kashmir stand exposed for what they are: bogus.

Lost Shangri La covers a wide range of subjects as becomes necessary to introduce a land that has been in dispute over the last five decades. The sub-title of the book is: *Glimpses of Ancient Kashmir*, which is exactly what this book is about. It re-creates a land once famous for its men of learning, where once the sound of Vedic recitation filled the Vale where now the swish of bullets rends the air. Kashmir, as the author depicts it, is a timeless wonder, the link between the past and the present still remaining unbroken despite all the turbulence it has witnessed over the years. It is the recounting of this unremitting cultural ethos that gives this work its special relevance. May it have a wide reading in India and abroad.

M.V. Kamath

Preface

THERE is hardly a literate or an illiterate person around the world who has not heard of Kashmir. Whether it is the newspaper or the radio or the television, it is been in the news ever since Kashmir acceded to India in 1947. Attention is centred around the fact that it is a Muslim majority State and Pakistan has been harping on the issue in all the world fora.

The popular image of Kashmir centres around this issue which in historic terms is of a temporary nature. Apart from the scenic beauty of Kashmir, the rest of India and the world do not know what ancient Kashmir was like.

The following pages are an attempt to give the reader an idea of what Kashmir was like — its kings, its polity, its people, its art, its literature, its governance and the overall picture of a Shangri La which was also cut off from the rest of the world, but which still had the 'La' through which trade and commerce passed.

This narrative is not a history nor does it claim to be based on history alone. It is a combination of facts, legend, folklore and impressions gathered from oral traditions which have come down the generations from person to person.

S. Sapru

James Hilton (1900-54), British novelist was born at Leigh, Lancashire, England. He toured Tibet in the 30s where he found the valley of Shangri La which is the name given to this book. This valley was practically cut off from the rest of the world and gave the author a unique peace of mind that resulted in the book *Lost Horizon* which he published in 1933. This was the period when an attempt was made to conquer Mount Everest. The famous British mountaineer Mallory led the expedition but was lost and no one knows whether he conquered Everest or not. It is still a mystery. James Hilton did not perhaps realise that the name Shangri La by itself with its prefix 'La' means a Mountain Pass. This valley that he described bears an uncanny resemblance to the Kashmir valley. Hence, the name.

Contents

1

The Killing Fields of Kashmir

HARDLY a day passes without news of Kashmir in the papers or the television, reminding us daily that a State called Jammu and Kashmir is in the grip of a turmoil only seen earlier hundreds of years ago, when Afghans and Pathans ruled the valley with the sword in one hand and the whip in the other.

Practically from the day India became independent, Kashmir has been in the news. Not only in the world fora, such as the UN and other international bodies, but down at the ground level as well when terrorism exploded like a time bomb, with the clatter of machine gun fire heard in all the corners of the valley spreading its tentacles like an octopus throughout the valley in the form of Kalakshinov culture from across the border. That Pakistan has fanned it, nurtured it, helped its growth does not need any elaboration. Pakistan has tried it in 1947, 1965, 1971 and even in 1999. When it found that it could not win on the battlefield, it resolved to what is in military parlance called 'Low Intensity Conflict'. What it implies in simple terms is terrorism, or bleeding a nation or a state slowly.

Terrorism, unlike politics, is the use of fear as a weapon. Terrorists have the freedom to strike where they want at will and when they want. Its victims are the ordinary folk, the population. By means of a killing spree — like spraying indiscriminately bullets in a busy market, they do not single out an individual — they spread fear. And when there is a possibility of people being organised or led by an individual, who could be a potential leader, they resort to selective individual killing or kidnapping. Fear spreads like a computer virus or even a virus of a dreaded disease. Then it is not fear of terrorism that drives people into submission, but fear itself.

That Is What Has Happened In Kashmir. And that is why many leaders today have security guards to ensure their physical safety. What terroists have not understood the world over is that a stage comes when the common people are attuned to it and beyond a certain point they cannot be driven into submission. Despite threats from militants, Kashmiris have gone out to vote in the recently held elections (1999).

Ideologically, a terrorist organisation needs a justification for killing. Either they resort to a dogma, like Marxism or to religion or even to race or language as the bedrock of their movement. Twisting a tenet of religion especially where people are mostly illiterate or already fanatic about their religious beliefs or even way of life, the terrorist is able to gain respectability in the eyes of the general public.

But the Achilles' heel of any terrorist or militant organisation is discipline. If discipline can be enforced, the organisation will eventually gain respectability, but when killings degenerate into rape and loot, then it results in anarchy. Compare the LTTE with the Kashmiri militants. In both cases, in the initial stages there was a mushrooming of different organisations, all aiming at the same objective, but LTTE through terror either eliminated rivals or rendered them impotent. But in Kashmir, there is a multiplicity of outfits.

Who calls the shots, who finances, who trains and who decides on targets, is the most important question for such movements. In the case of LTTE, it was home-grown, financed by and organised, armed and trained yes, by India earlier, but now on its own. But in the case of Kashmiri militants, the Pakistan government, with its vast resources, created the ISI specifically for Kashmir, though the Americans were told that it was for the fight against the Russians in Afghanistan.

When a movement is controlled from outside, by a third party, it invariably ends up in degenerating the movement. The initial aim and the final objective of the ISI was to drive out the non-Muslims from the Kashmir valley, although they are the oldest and original inhabitants of the State. Once, that objective was achieved, they realised that the Kashmiri Muslim though indoctrinated on fanatic beliefs, was not tough enough in their eyes to take on the paramilitary forces and the army. They decided that the now unemployed Afghan mercenaries who faced certain death in their own countries would be more suitable and amenable to control than the soft Kashmiri militants. Hence, the infiltration of mercenaries.

How long will the militancy in Kashmir last is the question everybody in India is asking. The answer to that lies in the proper understanding of the history of Kashmir.

Kashmir has been a pawn in the hands of kingdoms and countries, looters and plunderers, rulers and degenerates and when organised government was established, a brief spell of peace prevailed that was shattered in 1989, by a hail of gunfire and rivers of blood.

To understand Kashmir, one has to delve into the past — its history. Added to that one has to consider the geography. Tibet was once called the roof of the world and Kashmir the crossroad between continents and cultures. This will be confirmed if one looks closely at the map — to understand the geography and the terrain. And, history as well. Kashmir's history has been written literally by a sword dipped in blood.

But to understand, it is necessary to find out how Kashmir looked originally — that is at the beginning of time. Turmoil and violence came to the valley after the fourteenth century. Until then, Kashmir was literally cocooned and only the few summer months brought about the exchanges that made the valley and its people famous in the ancient world.

2

Beauty and Violence

IF you look carefully at the map of India, you will notice that the northern-most State of Jammu and Kashmir is shaped like a head. And the peninsula that the southern part of the country is, has the East and the West as its arms. So the country does look like someone you know — India. But right now the head has become a crucible and is burning furiously much to the shock and dismay of us all. Yet the fire started long ago and the embers have been hot and burning for the last forty years.

Kashmir — the name evokes images of snow-capped mountains, lush green forests, running streams, beautiful valleys and a peace loving people inhabiting it. You think of it when you want to go on your honeymoon, or even for a holiday. It is distant, it is beautiful, it is mysterious and it is friendly where one hears the cooing of birds and the laughter of children, where yellow flowers dot the countryside growing saffron, where one hears the singing of women working in the fields, where young boys used to assist their parents in ploughing the fields.

Today the silence of the night and the calm of the day are shattered by the rat-rat-rat of machine gun fire. Kalakshinovs have replaced toys, bombs have replaced footballs, weapons of all kinds are in use, and streets are getting covered with the blood of the innocent. The guns — where have they come from? Certainly not made in Kashmir. How much of blood has been spilt, is a matter of record, how much will be spilt is a question of time, but why should it be spilt. That no one is willing to answer.

Where one experienced first hand a mosaic of a composite culture, the ethos of Kashmiriat, that transcended the narrow confines of religion and caste or creed, where one associated the mild mannered Kashmiri Muslim youth to the desire to build a new Kashmir, one hears the strident harsh voices of Islamic fundamentalism that these young men have learnt 'across the line' that is Pakistan occupied Kashmir.

How did these voices which were gentle and soft change? Who got into their heads and filled them with hatred? Who made them obsessed with violence? And who hypnotised them to kill?

How long has Kashmir been in the news? As long as the Indian State has existed. That is when the country became independent on 15th August, 1947, there was no Kashmir problem. The Indian State was barely 69 days old when the problem started — 26th October, 1947, when the state acceded to India. Prior to that Pakistan unleashed Pathan tribals called 'Kabailis' on the helpless, defenceless valley. Since then we have come a long way. The Kashmir valley became a Kashmir issue — all the way from Srinagar, to Delhi, to New York at the United Nations, to the world capitals and recently to the UN Human Rights Commission meeting at Geneva. It was in the news. And what was the issue? A neighbouring country called Pakistan alleges that there are human rights violations in Kashmir and that the UN should send its inspectors to check and give a certificate. This from a country which has the worst human rights record in the region. Yet, because the people of Kashmir are majority Muslims, Pakistan has taken upon itself the task of defending Kashmiri Muslims, especially in world fora to embarrass India.

As you have heard, read and seen on the television, Pakistan despite making such an all-out effort to get a resolution passed, failed miserably. Even the members of the Organisation of Islamic Countries (OIC) did not support it.

So, Kashmir is burning and Pakistan is fuelling the fires. After having failed three times to conquer by war, it has unleashed terrorism across the border in the name of religion, indoctrinated and filled young people of Kashmir with the poison of fundamentalism, that has driven out the minority Hindus and Sikhs from the valley. They have become refugees in their own country, driven out from their homes and hearths at the point of a gun. And the diabolical part of it is that their leaders were selectively murdered in cold blood to make the minority community rudderless, leaderless and put fear in their hearts. They are with the majority Muslims, the original inhabitants of Kashmir and have an inalienable right to live there in peace and harmony. But Pakistan does not want that. Just as it tried in Punjab, by misleading and misguiding the youth, so also in Kashmir. In Punjab it has miserably failed. In Kashmir too, it will meet the same fate. Is that all there is to Kashmir? For millions of their countrymen in the four corners of India, this distant place brought daily into the living room by the television and the press, has become the symbol of secularism and a test case for the survival of the nation-state that is India, inhabited by people as diverse as diversity itself, separated, yet united by language, religion, geography, distance and ethnicity. Who are these Kashmiris, where did they come from, how do they live, what is their history and what is their future?

These are questions that need answers. Kashmir, as we all know is beautiful, but as the poet said like heaven, but we have been there. So, let us be content with what he said:

> If there be heaven on this earth, it is here, it is here, it is here.

Think about Heaven and the devil's schemes to convert it to hell. That is precisely what Pakistan is trying to do in Kashmir.

But that is another story.

3

Looking Closely at the Head

LEGEND has it that the Kashmir valley was in the beginning a vast mountain-lake called Satisar. Geological findings support this. Traces have been discovered of beaches on the sides of the surrounding hills and also fresh water fish, fossil oyster and black shells of water chest-nuts have been found embedded in layers in the earth at a height of 1,500 feet above the 5,000 level of the valley, proving its fluvial origin.

With so much of water around, it was but natural that someone would have to help drain it out for any civilisation to flourish. An ascetic namec Kashyapa Rishi reclaimed the land, which was called Kashyapa Mar (Kashyapa's abodė or stream), and later on this name was shortened to Kashmir. One finds in the books written several hundred years ago, and as late as nineteenth century that Kashmir was spelt by various European writers as Cashmere, which is also the usual English spelling for fabric.

Another version of the name has it that the name Kashmir is derived from the Sanskrit word *Ka* meaning water and *shmira* meaning to drain out.

While words might tally, it is the legend that lives on and has inspired generations of those who came after him till today, for it is said that it was Kashyapa Rishi's divine powers that drained the water filled valley. His disciples pleaded with him to save the land and he picked up a pebble and threw it on the water, which drained out, and the valley that is so famous today was formed.

The Jammu and Kashmir State has an area of 222,236 sq km a

large portion of, which is mountainous. About one-third of the area is under the illegal occupation of Pakistan and is known as the Pakistan-occupied Kashmir (POK). The main valley of Kashmir is 90 miles long and 40 miles wide. China has illegally occupied 37,555 sq km in the Aksai Chin area adjacent to Ladakh, in the eastern part of the State.

The population of the State as per the 1981 census (in 1991, no census was taken due to militancy, when minorities were driven out at the point of bayonets) was 5.99 million (approx. 60 lakh), but estimates show that the figure witl be higher keeping in view the increase in the decade of the eighties. While the literacy rate was 26.17 per cent, the Muslims are the biggest religious group in the Kashmir valley. There are Hindus, Sikhs, Buddhists and Christians as well, but most of the Hindus, the original inhabitants of the Kashmir valley, have been driven out and are living in refugee camps in Jammu, Delhi and other places in India.

The State of Jammu and Kashmir is a composite entity made up of six distinct regions: Jammu, Kashmir valley, Ladakh, Baltistan, Gilgit and Mirpur-Muzaffarabad region.

Three of these regions namely Baltistan, except Kargil, Gilgit and Mirpur-Muzaffarabad are under illegal Pakistani occupation since 1947. Of the remaining three regions. Kashmir valley which is predominantly Muslim is separated from the rest of the State by high Himalayan mountains, known as the Pir Panjal range which remains snow-bound for three to six months in a year.

That is why it has a distinct geographic, linguistic, ethnic and cultural identity of its own. It has all through the centuries remained a separate kingdom or a separate province of the various empires of India.

Kashmir valley is separated from Pakistan occupied territory of the State by the Uri-Titwal belt inhabited by Punjabi- and Pahari-speaking people who have little in common with the people of the valley.

Ladakh, except for Kargil, which has been joined to it since 1949 is predominantly Buddhist. It is linked with the Kishtwar area of Jammu in the south, Lahaul-Spiti area of Himachal Pradesh and Tibet in the east, Sinkiang province of China in the north and Baltistan now occupied by Pakistan in the west.

Aksai Chin, now under Chinese occupation was part of Ladakh. Siachen Glacier, lies between Baltistan and Ladakh and converges on Leh, the capital of Ladakh. Leh has been linked with Chandigarh by air and a motorable road passing through Himachal Pradesh. There is another road link, which connects Srinagar via Sonamarg to Leh, but this road is closed to traffic for almost six months in the year due to snow and landslides.

Jammu, the home of Dogras is predominantly Hindu and the place is geographically in the plains. It stretches from Pathankot in Punjab to the Banihall Pass in the Pir Panjal range of mountains en route to Srinagar. It has a population of about 40 lakh, nearly 30 per cent of which are displaced Muslims from Pakistan-occupied-Kashmir. The unity amidst diversity syndrome can best be seen in the State. The people from the valley speak Kashmiri, those from Jammu Dogri, the Ladakhis speak the Tibetan derived Ladakhi language, while the Uri-Muzaffarabad people speak Punjabi.

Jammu is the link between Kashmir valley and the rest of the country. This then is a close look at the head that you see on the map — the State of Jammu and Kashmir. The regions are different, the people are different, but they are all citizens of India and that of Jammu and Kashmir State.

4

A Seat of Ancient Learning

KASHMIR was from the earliest times (details about which have been chronicled), a seat of iearning. From the records and writings of the period we learn about three levels of learning and the depth of knowledge of the men who disseminated learning. Discussion was one of the most important modes of learning at that time. Whether it was metaphysics or dialectical materialism or medical sciences, the stress was on memory and discussions. Arguments and debates were common and out of it would emerge criticism and commentary that is essential in chronicling the views of any civilisation.

Famous ancient Chinese travellers, like Hieun Tsiang and Du-Kong, who visited Kashmir and engaged themselves in studying the culture by learning the local literary language namely Sanskrit did so about the year AD 631 and 759 respectively.

It was a sign of the times that no scholar could be considered learned enough till he had associated himseif with the illustrious learned men in Kashmir for several years and taken lessons from them. The comparison might be odious, but the value that we in India attached to and still attach to a foreign degrees from Britain or the United States or Germany or France is similar perhaps to the need during ancient times to get a certification in scholarship by learning in Kashmir. Perhaps in those times the bio-data of a scientist or a scholar was determined by whether an entry called "Kashmir" was in it or not.

Writes Hieun Tsiang:

The people of Kashmir love learning and are well cultured.

> Since centuries learning has been held in great respect in 'Kashmir'.

Al-Beruni, who accompanied Mohammed Ghaznavi to Punjab in AD1021 wrote,

> Kashmir is the high school of Indian sciences.

People came from far and near countries in search of Sanskrit learning here and many amongst them, charmed by the congenial climate and natural beauty settled down there.

The physical features of the valley and its mountain barriers kept many an invader off, many a marauder off and left the valley and its people in peace.

Says Pandit Anand Koul, father of the famous Kashmiri writer, P.N.K. Bamzai, in his monumental work *The Kashmiri Pandit*,

> behind its natural boundaries the republic enjoyed immunity from foreign aggression and therefore people from other countries swarmed there.

Al-Beruni says:

> The victory of Punjab by Mohammed Ghaznavi made people fly away to places where our hands cannot yet reach to Kashmir, Benares and other places.

Poet and historian Kalhana wrote in 1149:

> Such is Kashmir, the country which may be conquered by the force of spiritual merit but not by armed force . . . where there are no baths in winter, comfortable landing places on the river banks, where the rivers being free from aquatic animals are without peril; where realising that the land created by his father is unable to bear heat, the hot-rayed sun honours it by bearing himself with softness even in summer. Learning, high dwelling houses, saffron, iced water, grapes and the like — what is common place, that is difficult to secure in paradise.

The famous explorer and writer Francis Younghusband.

> The beautiful Greece, with its purple hills and varied contour, its dancing seas and clear blue sky, produced the graceful Greeks. But Kashmir is more beautiful than Greece. It has the same blue sky and brilliant sunshine, but its purple hills are on a far grander scale and if it has no sea, it has lake and river and the still more impressive snowy mountains. It has too greater variety of natural scenery, of field and forest of rugged mountains and open valleys. And to me who has seen both countries, Kashmir seems much the more likely to impress a race by its natural beauty. Has it ever made any impression? Are there no remains of buildings, roads, aquaducts, canals, statues or any such mark by which a people leaves its impress on a country? And is there any literature or history?

Ancient civilisations leave their imprints on the sands of time, and it is either by writings or by physical remains of buildings, etc., that one can understand the soul of a civilisation. Certainly there are ruins of temples and buildings all over the valley, remarkable for their Egyptian solidity, simplicity and durability, as well as for what Cunningham describes as their graceful elegance, the massive boldness of their parts and the happy propriety of their outlines.

And Kashmir has the unique distinction of possessing an unbroken historical record from ancient times to the present day. In the field of literature and philosophy, its record stands second to none in the rest of India, says PNK Bamzai in his book, *A History of Kashmir*.

For upward of 2000 years, Kashmir has been the home of Sanskrit learning and from this small valley have issued masterpieces of history, poetry, romance, fable and philosophy. Kashmiris are proud and justly proud of the literary glories of their land. For centuries, it was the home of the greatest Sanskrit scholars and at least one great Indian religion. Shaivism has found some of its most eloquent teachers on the banks of the Vitasta — the ancient name for the river that flows through present-day Srinagar and is known by the name of Jhelum river. Some of the greatest Sanskrit poets were born and wrote in the valley and from it has issued in the Sanskrit language a world famous collection of folklore, says Grierson, a European scholar.

Rishi Kashyap

5

Where did the Kashmiris Come From?

AFTER Kashyapa Rishi drained out the valley, that bears his name, he needed people to inhabit it. The pre-historic period as mentioned in both the *Nilmat Purana* and *Rajatarangini* shows that Brahmans were brought there by Kashyapa Rishi. They were penitents and philosophers, living apart from the world and its temptations and entirely engrossed in the pursuit of knowledge, leading the lives of introspection and practising the lives of purity.

They sojourned in the valley during summer, performing austere penance in the cool climate and returned to where they came from on the approach of the winter. In those times, there lived three tribes called *Nagas, Pishachas* and *Yakshas*, who used to go to Tibet in summer and return to Kashmir in winter. They were evidently aboriginies. Aboriginies, as we know by definition are original or native inhabitants of a country and in the case of Kashmir in pre-historic times, the Brahmans who inhabited the valley were its original inhabitants.

It is but natural that being ascetics and peace loving that the Brahmans used to initially out of fear perhaps depart from the valley before the arrival of the three tribes, from Tibet. In course of time, the Brahmans began to reside there permanently.

It will, thus, be clear that the Kashmiri Brahmans were quite distinct as a race from the aboriginal tribes and other immigrants. They retained a separate way of life. They were generally followers of the Shaiva philosophy. This religious system was in ancient times, the subject of much study among the scholars. Their teachings have in fact influenced the entire Indian peninsula from Kashmir to Kanya-

Kumari. Though Shaivite in belief Vaishnavism is also read, practised and respected. *Avataras* of Vishnu are worshipped in temples. Each family was devoted to the worship of one or another of the four goddesses, namely Sharika, Rajnh, Jvala and Bala. They followed as they do even now, the *Sanatana Dharma*.

Rajatarangini, the most authoritative history of Kashmir says that it is certain that the Kashmiri Brahman came from a colony of Aryan immigrants from Central Asia. Their features and fair complexion indicated that they are from Aryan race.

The Aryans were a long headed race of tall stature with narrow noses and fair complexion. Their purest representatives are found today mainly in Kashmir.

Sir Mortimer-Williams in his book *Modern India and Indians* writes: The Kashmiri Pandits are among the finest types of the Aryan race" and George Campbell in his book *Ethnology of India* says that the Kashmiri Brahmans are quite high Aryan in the type of their features very fair and handsome, with high chiselled features and no trace of inter mixture of the blood of any other race. It may be partly race and partly occupation but they certainly have a greater refinement and regularity of features than the Afghans and others. The high nose, slightly aquiline, but by no means what we call Jewish or nut cracker, is a common type. Raise a little brow of a Greek statue and give the nose a small turn at the bony point in front of the bridge, so as to break the straightness of line, you have then the model type of this part of INDIA, to be found in the living men and in the statues dug up in the Peshawar valley.

The average Kashmiri is strong and atheletic. But none of them are martial and the Brahmans are in this respect no exception. They rule by the brain and the pen and not by the sword and certainly not guns today as the imported cult of violence from Pakistan is tearing the valley apart. Kashmir did centuries ago belong to the Kabul kingdom (Afghanistan). But it was never in any degree colonised by the Afghans, whose rulers preferred to keep it apart, not wanting to admit any other subjects, who might not wish to leave once they settle down there.

Pocock, a historian, says that there are traces of the settlements of Kashmiris in Greece and from this is he infers that the Kashmiri Pandits were originally Greek or Persian settlers in the valley, who were brahmanised. It is quite possible that some Kashmiris went to Persia and Greece during the time of Darius Hystapse's invasion of the, Punjab and Alexander's conquest of India in 331 BC and settled there. Hence there might be tracess of settlements in these countries pointing to the Kashmiri connection. The tribe of *mlecchas* which existed in Kashmir during the reign of Ashoka is assumed to have been Greeks, who were driven out of the valley by his son Jalauka. This is mentioned in the *Rajatarangini.*

Wherever, they came from, it is certain that they were in the valley. In pre-historic times, or when the age of writing and records came, they were already scholars and learned men. Their origins are known though the modern definitive way of identification may not be able to do so. Who they were is a matter of curiosity, but what they did is a matter of history.

We have mentioned about the origins of Kashmiri Brahmans, but like all males, we have mainly talked in terms of the masculine gender. Lest we be accused of gender bias, it is relevant to relate a small tale if only to illustrate that the home maker that a woman is, did not confine herself to the four walls of her home and her contribution too needs to be recorded.

If the men had aquiline noses, so did the women. They were beautiful, no doubt about it. But like women, everywhere they also produced heroines. Kashmiri women have distinguished themselves in ancient times. As queens with executive powers, as writers, grammarians and even poets. Who has not heard of Lalishwari, whose poems are still sung in the twenty-first century.

But back to the tale. She was a queen. Her name is lost in antiquity. But when she had her baby in her lap, foreign ambassadors were sitting in her court. She brought the baby along and fed it in their presence. One of the ambassadors was bold enough to ask:

> Your Majesty, you have so many maids, can't anyone of the them feed the baby.

Yes, I do have them, but my baby will become the king one day. And he has to be fed by his mother.

You see even a Queen has to be a mother to her child.

In the whole of India, Brahmans are labelled as Brahmans but curiously enough the Brahmans of Kashmir are called *pandits*. Many people wonder why. Dr. Gauri Bazaz Malik has discussed it in a letter to Koshur Samachar, the organ of the Kashmiri *pandit* community.

Who were these people and from where they came to occupy the Valley for the first time. There are different views to explain this phenomenon. It is believed that they were all Aryans and the progeny of Kashyapa Rishi and as such they were all Brahmans.

A deep study of the Vedic scriptures would reveal that, in ancient times, only Brahmans used to go to such secluded spots in the mountains and in thick forests far away from worldly pleasures and other allurements for single-minded concentration to seek knowledge and to perform deep meditation for attaining high levels of spiritualism. Moreover, a Brahman was then regarded as the personification of learning and wisdom, serenity and purity. He was supposed to be the custodian of knowledge, which reveals the ultimate truth, i.e., God. He was to be the nectar of mankind and embodiment of the truth and placed on a very high pedestal in society.

According to history, the Hindu rule in the Valley came to an abrupt end in AD 1320. and after that the conversion of Hindus began. In the *Rajatarangini* written by Kalhana, the existence of castes like Brahmans, Kshatriyas, Vaishyas and Shudras is clearly mentioned in it during the Hindu rule in Kashmir. However, at some point of time between the establishment of the Muslim rule in the fourteenth century and a few decades after its end in the early first century, the hierarchy of Hindu castes in Kashmir got finished with mass conversions at the point of sword. By the middle of the nineteenth century, the only remaining portion of the former Hindu caste system of Kashmir and the only Hindus who had their origin in Kashmir were the Kashmiri *Pandits*. Being the people of superior caste, they resisted the conversion very rigidly and in the process paid a very high price for it, while the other caste groups embraced Islam to save their souls.

Shri Balraj Madhok has written much on the history and culture of Kashmir. According to him, the term *pandit* was given to Kashmiri Brahmans by the Moghul rulers of Delhi through a decree as they used to have a great command over Persian which was the court language at that time. This was done to differentiate Kashmiri Brahmans from the Brahmans of the plains, who had no knowledge of Persian and were only well-versed in Sanskrit which was of no use for getting entry in the Moghul durbar, says Dr. B.N. Sharga, President, Kashmiri Association, Lucknow.

Lt. Col.R.K. Langar says: 'The meaning of the word *pandit* has to be understood in its correct perspective. Ordinarily *pandit* is a person who is well-versed in languages, scriptures, literature, poetry, oratory and logic. Bu this definition of a *pandit* is not comprehensive. In its complete sense, a *pandit* is primarily a man of wisdom, more than just being a scholar. A scholar need not be a man of wisdom even though he is fully credited with scholarly works. A scholar can become a man of wisdom with his self-effort if he raises himself above bookish knowledge. Thus, a *pandit* is a person who has raised himself beyond the regions of birth, language and literature. He is a man of values and morally upright who looks upon all with an equal and compassionate eye. From the spiritual point of view, a *pandit* has freed himself from desire and personal ego. Hence, any person possessing these qualities can be addressed as a *pandit* whether he belongs to Kashmir or any other part of the world.

In *Bhagavad Gita*, the word *pandit* has been described at three places, in chapter 2, verse 11; in Chapter 4, verse 19 and in chapter 5, verse 18. It describes him as a *jnani* who has burnt all actions in the fire of knowledge. As per the *Gita*, a *pandit* is one who has attained the knowledge of *atma* and has received the grace of God. There cannot be a better authority than the *Gita* on differentiating words and their true meanings.

The other major point raised is the usage of the word Brahman in its implications when prefixed with the word Kashmiri. First, I agree with the learned writer that Shaivism of Kashmir, like Buddhism and Vedanta do not believe in the caste system. As per Kashmir Shaivism, there is no difference between caste, colour and creed. Buddhism and Vedanta alsio do not recognise the caste system by birth or the hereditary caste system; which is being followed in our country. As per the Vedantic thought, a Brahman is one who is pure and has knowledge and realisation.

The *Gita* divides men as per their mental capabilities and these are termed as castes. These are not based on birth but on an individual's ability (verses 41 to 44 of chapter 18). A person born in a Brahman family is not a Brahman if he does not display Brahman-like qualities. This concept of caste system has to be understood in totality to remove any misconception of the system. The other thing which has to be understood clearly is that a *pandit* is one who has risen above the modes of nature or *gunas*, whereas a Brahman has an abundance of *satvika* qualities which is the highest rung of the ladder of the *gunas*.

Kashmiri-speaking Hindus are addressed as *pandits* because, in one way or the other, they are connected with the sages and self-realised persons of Kashmir and they are carrying with them this mantle and title. As we know, Kashmir has produced a number of saints and sages who had tremendous influence in society and the people took great pride in calling them their ancestors. Conversely, we can have Kashmiri-speaking Kshatriyas, Vaishyas and Shudras if such people display non-Brahman qualities of other castes, not by birth but by their capabilities.

Lastly, a priest is also called a *guru* when he conducts a religious ceremony.

Dr. Gauri Bazaz Malik adds: speaking on this subject I recall a National Seminar on The Human Rights of Minorities, Scheduled Castes/Scheduled Tribes and Woman in Mumbai on 10th December, 10,1998, on the occasion of 'the Golden Jubilee of the United Nations Declaration of Human Rights'.

I chose to speak on 'Women of Kashmir'. At the end of my presentation, I was put a very pertinent question by a few bright young men. They asked me " why did you repeatedly use the term *pandit* while referring to the Hindus of Kashmir, why not Brahman?" My immediate response was that 'it is a habit of *samskara*'. I told them that, though I am not an ,expert on the subject, I could, however, offer my impressions. The Eclectic Trika Shaivism of Kashmir like Buddhism and Samkhya Yoga does not believe in the caste system. It is a philosophy based on Shiva-Shakti concept. At most of the important festivals of the *pandits* like *Shivratri*, no icons of the *avtaras* but a collection of symbois (*yantras*) of Shiva-*cum*-Shakti get worshipped. In fact, it is the priest, called *Brahman*, who conducts the ceremony. He is called *guruji* while the *yajmana* is a *pandit* or a *bhatt*. As a group also, the *pandits* refer to themselves as *bhatts*.

Someone from the audience, helpfully, remarked 'In Kashmir, some Muslims also are called *pandits*'. 'That is right and supports my proposition', I replied, 'After all, *pandit* means a scholar and an authority on a subject. During Sultan Zain-ul-Abidin's (*Badshah*) time, Hindus as Persian scholars continued to be addressed as *pandits*. It has to be noted that Trika (Shaivism), Buddhism and Sufism do not divide or segregate humanity into different castes,' I added.

6

A Symbol of India's Cultural Unity

NOTHING perhaps brings out in bold relief the picture of the unity of India from time immemorial than the cultural fabrique of ancient Kashmir. Whatever may have been the political situation, changing as it was from time to time when kings and adventurers decided the fate of nations, the remarkable fact of the oneness of the country has to be seen to be understood. Despite its geographical isolation, this valley played a vital role in enriching the cultural life which pulsated throughout the length and breadth of India. The Indo-Aryan immigrants, who Kashmiris were, having settled there, developed their inherited Vedic art and culture, to an extent that it remains there even today.

Says PNK Bamzai:

> The first historical figure that stands out in *Rajatarangini* of course is Ashoka the Great, who brought the valley and the neighbouring area under his vast empire.

He not only visited the valley, but also sent out Buddhist missionaries, thus, making Kashmir in a short time the fountain-head of Mahayana Buddhism and advance post of Indian Culture. Later during Kaniska's reign, missionaries were sent to Central Asia and China carrying with them the Doctrine of the Buddha to these countries. Links in the field of art and culture were, thus, established with other centres in India.

A number of celebrated Buddhist scholars made the valley their headquarters. Among them were the celebrated Nagarjuna, Ashvagosha, Vasubandhu and Sharmatrata. It may seem quite normal and ordinary today for a teacher from Trivandrum University to go to Srinagar University. But consider the times in that era and even in historic times, the distances involved and the mode of transport. Kashmirian Buddhist scholars were in those times adorning the teaching and research departments at Vikaramashila and Nalanda Universities. How Sanskrit came to Kashmir is lost in antiquity. Originally from the Indo-Aryan belt, they did inherit a tradition and no tradition can be passed on without a language. Hence, Sanskrit, which helped to cement the bond with the rest of the country by its systematic study and propagation, became the link. It is not, thus, surprising to find that all the literature produced in Kashmir on Buddhism was in Sanskrit. And it is not hard to imagine a constant two-way flow of scholars from Kashmir to the rest of the country and vice versa.

At a time when Pali was the language of writing in the rest of India, especially during Ashoka's reign, we find that Buddhist literature was written in Sanskrit. A very important part in this work was done by Kumarajiva and his band of Kashmiri Buddhist scholars and as a result of this, Kucha became a centre of Sanskrit learning in Central Asia. During this century a large number of Sanskrit manuscripts written on birch-bark have been discovered in the vast regions of Central Asian uplands and the only lot of Sanskrit Buddhist manuscripts ever discovered in India has come from Gilgit in Kashmir.

Apart from students, scholars and teachers coming to the valley for higher studies, pilgrims came from Central Asia and China. Hieun-Tsang spent two years in the valley studying Buddhist texts in Sanskrit and so did the earlier scholars Che-mong and Pa-yong. Ou-kong, another scholar spent four years in Kashmir and studied Sanskrit and Vinaya from three teachers.

During Ashoka's time, Sanskrit was written both in the Kharoshthi and the Brahmana script in Kashmir. The scholars developed a script of their own the — SARADA — which though differing from the Devanagari in details follows it in its essentials. Surprising as this may sound, the Tibetans, who did not have a script for their language, adopted the Sarada script in the ninth century AD. Birch-bark was widely used for both literary writings and Government correspondence and commercial transactions. It was also used for packing parcels and lining roofs to make them watertight. Even today one can find houses in the valley built in the old style having birch-bark lining and an earthen roof. During winter with snow, hail and rains, there was no leakage of water into the rooms. The ink is used for writing on birch-bark was prepared by a special process so that it might not get faded or washed off by water. Birch-bark, as any scientific investigation will show, is not attacked by dampness. This way many old manuscripts were hidden in wells and pits and escaped destruction at the hands of many an ignorant and unscrupulous ruler.

Kashmir had a large number of what we would today call specialised colleges or universities. Whether it was a temple which by our ancient tradition was the centre of all activities in India, or a library, which automatically made it a centre for learning, occupied the pride of place in having a large number of libraries of Sanskrit manuscripts. "Temples and Viharas were the repositories of these literary treasures, but there were huge private libraries too maintained by families having literary traditions", says historian *pandit* Anand Koul.

Even as late as 1876, when George Bahier, the European scholar, went to Kashmir in search of Sanskrit manuscripts, and when Sanskrit learning there was not as flourishing as in ancient times, he found more than 22 Sanskrit-speaking Kashmiri *pandits* as well as traders and officials who were possessors of the most considerable collections of manuscripts.

The cultural unity of India was there always and Kashmir was a beautiful symbol of it. Imagine a man sitting in Kanyakumari, 2600 years ago when literacy in modern parlance was unknown, talking of going to Kashi or a man sitting at Kurukshetra talking of going to Rameswaram. They did it, they learnt about each other and they bound the nation by an invisible string that modern folk call national unity or identity. Neither language, nor geography has made any difference. They may look different, like the Kashmiri does, but contrary to some modern beliefs, they are the same, and the nation they hail from has borne different names from ancient times and today is called Bharat or as the Europeans have called it, India.

7

Centres of Excellence

DURING the Middle Ages, Heidelberg, a small town in Prussia (now known as Germany) became a seat of learning. Recently it celebrated its 600th anniversary. Oxford is also considered an old university and by modern standards so is Harvard. But look at Taxila, Nalanda and Martand and Nagarjuna.

To give you an idea, Taxila (now in Pakistan) and Nalanda (Bihar) and Martand (Kashmir) belong to the BC era. By that one means that they were there before Christ or the Christian era. But arithmetically speaking the Christian era is only 2000 years old and our civilisation dates back to the pre-historic times. When one looks at the ruins, the excavations, one marvels at the skill and the accuracy with which huge stones were carved, sculptures were made and materials were mixed with ancient tools and modern skills. They did not have cranes, bulldozers or theodolites or sophisticated laboratories. Yet they have left behind examples of the best in skills. Whether it is art, architecture, literature, poetry and drama the search was an eternal one. Right through the centuries, the scale was merit and in search of excellence students traversed the length and breadth of the country.

A man in the north did come to the south and one in the east did go to the west, all of them in search of knowledge. Ask anyone today: Where do you get knowledge and he will tell you, school, college and the university. Today the system is organised to suit the modern age. Then it was organised to suit the needs of the time.

Martand — the name echoes images of grandeur on a superlative scale, the architecture, the blending of the lines, the utilitarian way of planning and the built-in atmosphere to promote learning. Do buildings make universities or promote knowledge. No, stones can be made to speak, but knowledge needs human hands and human brain to develop and transmit from one to the other, from the *guru* to the *shishya*.

What we have are the remains of Martand — a temple, with scholars in residence. A temple in ancient times was not only a centre of religious rites, but also the cultural hub of the community. The entire life of the community was centred round the temple and without perhaps realising it the people found what they were looking for. Mental peace in front of God, the religious sanction for any action, training for priesthood, learning Sanskrit and even mundane but important aspect of life-matrimonial match-making.

So when we talk of ancient Hindu temples, we must remember, that they were colleges, schools and universities ail rolled into one.

Speaking of Martand, this noble ruin is the most striking in size and position of all the existing remains. The temple itself is not more than 40 feet tall, but its solid walls and bold outlines towering over the fluted pillars of the surrounding colonnades, give it an imposing appearance.

The mass of buildings consists of one lofty central edifice with a small-detached wing on each side of the entrance, the whole standing in a quadrangle, surrounded by a column made of fluted pillars with intervening trefoil headed recesses. The length of the outer wall, which is blank, is about 90 yards, that of the front is 60 yards. There are in all eighty-four columns, a singularly appropriate number in a temple of the sun. If as is supposed the number 84 is considered sacred by the Hindus in consequence of its being the product of the number of days in a week and the number of signs in the zodiac. It is thought that the whole of the interior of the quadrangle was originally filled with water to a level up to one foot of the base of the columns and that access to the temple was gained by a raised pathway of slabs supported on the solid blocks at short intervals which connected the gateway flight of steps with that leading to temple. A constant supply of fresh water was kept up through a canal from the River Lidder that was conducted alongside of the mountain for service of the village close by. In the centre of either side of the longer interior chamber is a window reaching the floor and about eight feet high. The walls, thus, divided quarterly are filled with single figures in relief, two of Surya and of Lakshmi, one of each panel.

What is most impressive about Martand is its overwhelming size, some degree of optical illusion and complete harmony of the buildings and of their decoration and figure sculptures.

Dr. Herman Goetz, a German expert on art and letters says:

> Martand stands not quite isolated. It has a smaller counterpart in the plains, the temple of Malot in the salt range. Malot raised the problems of Martand temples even more acutely. For it has a cascade of the purely Roman and Corinthian Half pillars enclosing trifollated archways crowned by a set of the high *sikharas*. If the first (Martand) was proved characteristics for Lalitaditya's region, the second (Malot) was possible only in a time of the closest contact with Bihar and Bengal, that is when king of Gauda had become Lalitaditya's vassal.

There are other Temples like Pandrenthan and Shankaracharya, to name but a few. They were centres of learning of excellence but more of that later.

8

Their Literary and Artistic Achievements

THE study and development of Sanskrit language was an object of special study in ancient Kashmir. They made important contribution to the study of Vedic literature, grammar and philology. For instance, Ubbatbhasa is a learned exposition of text of *Sukla-Yajurveda*.

Panini's monumentai work on Sanskrit grammar, *The Ashtadhyi*, was commented upon by Patanjali in his *Mahabhashya*, a work of unrivalled importance on grammar. Incidentally, Patanjali is said to have lived in the second century BC and the Kashmiri tradition upheld by several scholars claims him as having been born in the village of Godra in the south Kashmir.

The study of *Mahabhashya* received a setback towards beginning of first century AD. Kalhana refers to a similar restoration of the study of Patanjali's great grammatical work under the Jayapida. His teacher in grammar Kshirasvamin, son of Ishvarsvamin, wrote his well-known commentary on the Dhatupatha or the study of verbs and other grammatical treatises still extent.

That Kshirasvamin was a Kashmiri is proved by a passage in the *Vamsastuti* appended by Rajanama Ananda to his commentary on the *Naisadhcharita* (composed in 1654) where he is claimed to be one of the great Scholars produced by the Rajanaka family of Kashmir along with Kayatta, Uvatta and Mamatha. Kayatta, son of Jayatta and a brother ol Mamatha has also given us *Mahabhashya Pradeepa*, a guide to study of *Mahabhashya*.

Another commentary on Pannini's work *Kashikavritti*, written jointly by Jayaditta and Vamana, two Kashmiri grammarians has been mentioned by I-tsing in the seventh century AD. Two other Kashmiri grammarians, Bhatta, of. Baghuveritti, Jagadhara, the author of *Balabodhini* and Chiku Bhatta of *Baghuvritti*, propagated the teachings of the Katantra School, which though founded outside Kashmir had many adherents in the valley.

In metrics and prosody Kashmiri authors have made valuable contribution to Sanskrit language and literature. Pinglacharya, the author of the well known work on the metrics, Pingala, was a Kashmiri and so was Kedarbhatta who wrote *Vrittaratnakara*, used widely after Pingala. Another work on metrics Suvritta-Tilaka was the work of the well-known Kashmiri author Kshemendra. Mamatta his later contemporary wrote a book *Savdavyaparacharcha*. In the field of lexicography also Kashmir's contribution is considerable. The *Anekarthakosa* of Mankha is of special importance and is an improvement on preceding authors like Amarasimha. The latter's work was commented upon by Kshirasvamin in his treatise entitled *Narmalinganushasanam*.

Poetics: Both according to their own account and those of the learned men in India, the Kashmiris were in ancient times as distinguished in the *Alankara-Shastra* or poetics as in the poetry and produced a long series of writers on the subjects. Looking at the surrounding in which the poets worked, Mother nature's bounties in full in front of them, it is no wonder that the accent was necessarily on the pursuit of beauty in all respects. The Kashmiri writers did not only develop some of the earlier schools of the poetics that were born in other parts of India such as *rasa*, *alankara*, *riti*, *vakrokti* and *aucitya* but made original contribution to the science of the poetics with their theory of the *dhvani*.

The Rasa School, based on Bharata (Natyshastra) found its exponent in Lollata, contemporary of king Jayapida (ninth century AD), Sankulika, his contemporary ,improved upon Lollata's theory that *rasa* belonged to the performer only, by explaining that it was related to the spectator as well. Abhinavagupta's definition of *rasa* is that his magnification meaning thereby that Almighty God is also involved in it. As was the prevalent custom then, literary works were often connected with legend and religion, ritual and theory, and customs and habits of the time.

Bhatta Udbhatta, the court *pandit* of the king Jayapida wrote profusely on the Alankara School. His *Kavyalankaravritti*, now lost and *Alankara-samgraha* deal in detail with the definition and explanation of the forty-one *alamkaras*. Rudratta (ninth century AD) reviews the whole field of the poteics in the sixteen chapters of his monumental work, *Kavyalankara*.

The Riti School had its exponents in Vamana, a minister of Jayadipa. In his work *Kavyalankara-sutra*, he asserts that *riti* is the soul or poetry. He was the first to distinguish between *guna* and *alankara* and, thus, his work is an improvement on Dandin.

But it is for their theory of *dhvani*, a unique contribution to the science of the poetics that the Kashmiri authors deserve credit. The first profounder of this school was Anandavardhana who in his *Dhvanyaloka* asserts that it is *dhvani* that is the soul of poetry. According to Kane:

> The *Dhvanyaloka* is an epoch-making work in the history of *alankara* literature. It occupies the same position in the poetics as Panini's *Ashtadhyayi* in grammar and Shankaracharya's commentary on Vedanta.

9

Aesthetics — The Fragrance of Life

ABHINAVAGUPTA, was a famous poet, critic, philosopher and saint of Kashmir who wrote profusely on aesthetics, in the tenth century AD. Like a drama moving to its climax, aesthetics thought in Kashmir moved to its highest point in the history of the Indian aesthetics. He was one of the those very few Individuals who have earned as much reverence for the humility of their character as for the magnitude of their intellectual capacity.

Even now (not since 1990), when the gun came to the valley and those who were his descendants and followers were cruelly, inhumanly driven out of the valley). His name is uttered by unlettered villagers in Kashmir with the deepest respect. It is believed that near the villages of the Magam on the Gulmarg road, he 'entered *samadhi*' with 1200 disciples. Incidentally, Magam has been in the news for militant and security forces clashes in very recent times. What would Abhinavagupta have said, one shudders to think of.

He was born sometime between AD 950 and 960 in a family of scholars. His ancestors Atrigupa, a reputed scholar of Kanauj, came to Kashmir at the invitation of the King Lalitaditya, and settled permanently in valley.

Abhinavagupta's grandfather Varahaputa and his father Narasinghaputa, were both well known for their vast learning. From his mother Vimalakala, he inherited a deep interest in spiritualism.

But he lost his mother during his childhood and his father renounced the world thereafter. But spurred on by a steely determination he pursued his studies

With zeal, he was fortunate enough to have among his teachers versatile people. Some of them were versed in Buddhist lore and scripture, others were Jains, while still others Shaivites. He studied metaphysics, poetry, and aesthetics and took lessons in practical *yoga*. After mastering these vital branches of knowledge, the creative phase of his life began. He studied all the tantric texts from the point of view of Kashmir Saivism and the result of his labour was his famous *Tantraloka*. In his second phase, he made a study of all the schools of the poetics and produced his famous work *Aesthetics, Abhinavabharati and Locana*, a commentary on Anandavardhana's *Dhvanyaloka*. In the third and final phases of his life, he was drawn towards metaphysical problems and made his own important formulation which raised Kashmir Shaiva philosophy to the highest level and secured for it a permanent place in the history of human thought.

He remained a celibate throughout his life and in his later years virtually became an ascetic. This, however, observes Dr. V. S. Narvane, should not give the impression that he was far removed from the domain of practical human experience. He remained in the domain through his extraordinary memory vvhich enabled him to carry in his mind all the impressions he had gathered from books, conversations with teachers and friends and his own experience.

His works abound with references to joy and sorrows of human life. At a time, when Botany as a subject was not known or developed, he showed an interest in flora and fauna of the valley and sings with joy and beauty of the Vitatsa (the river Jhelum) meandering slowly through paddy fields and orchards and trees and villages of Kashmir. The liberal tradition, the kinds of wine brewed in Kashmir and talks of the physical beauty of women of Kashmir. In him we find the ultimate sage, scholar and many contributions to poetics. He took his education at Varanasi. His famous work *Kavyaprakasha* possesses such merit that it has been commented upon by more than a century by ancient and modem scholars. It covers the whole gambit of rhetoric, deals with merits and demerits of poetry, the functions of different words and their sources and speech and champions schools of poetics. After his death, the tenth chapter of *Kavyaprakasha* was continued by his pupil Allata Manikyachandra who has written the first and most reliable commentary on *Kavyaprakasha*. Rajanaka Ruyyaka, who lived in the twelfth century AD wrote *Alankaravasav* and ably summarised the views of early writers.

While in every field there are the leaders who shine in their own glory the critic two centuries later begins to evaluate the work of the intellectuals of an age, finds the task easy as specialisation in those hoary days was clear and overlapping taken in stride. Today the same things is called a multi-disciplinary approach or a macro or synoptic view of the world. To the modern generation, the aesthetics may not mean much in concrete terms, but it can never be far from us, though we may not recognise it either through thoughtlessness indifference. Aesthetics adds meaning to life, zest for living and a desire to strive for that perfection that every human being strives for and that is what the Kashmiri writers and thinkers did. History judged and evaluated them, but over the passage of centuries, they are being treated with extinction. This is a part of our national heritage, we should not lose it.

10

Folklore is the Spice of Life

FOLK and fable; these two intrinsically linked to man's imagination in putting together legends, facts, and fancy and produce from it literature of a different kind. Folklore will always differ from region to region. You could nok find a reminder that Santa Claus drives on in a land, which had Krishna and Arjuna, Rama and Lakshmana riding the chariot. It is local, it is regional, it reflects daily life, it mirrors fast happenings, real or imagined. Facts merge with what we may call fiction and produce legends folklore. It is a mixture of fact and fantasy, but it does a historical base of Kashmir's a long tradition of story telling. Remember this was before birch-bark writing or palm-leaf writing which was meant for the scholars only, and certainly before paper. Stories were told and retold and passed on from father to son, mother to daughter to keep alive the invisible thread called culture and heritage. And then folklore become history, the scholars took a hand and recorded it.

One could ask why Kashmir had such a strong base in folklore. Was it because the valley was cut off for more than seven to eight months in a year with all the passes blocked. There was no other source of amusement and with the temperature below zero it is by natural that after having ensured that the shelter above one's head was secure, people would take interest in stories listening and telling.

Whatever might be the reasons, some of the world's best known tales have originated in Kashmir. This is not known even today, because centuries of neglect have practically wiped of Kashmir from the cultural, literary sea in a large measure. Priority in those days was survival stark and physical from the sword of the invader.

Apart from Gunadhya's legendary *Brihat-katha*, which is no longer existing and Somadeva's *Brihatkatha-sagara*, many collections of stories were produced among which Kshemendra's *Brihatkatha-manjari* and a version of *Panchatantra* known as *tantrakhayusada* are particularly significant.

Somadeva was one of the founders of fiction writing and his work has reached the remotest corners of the world in one form or other. He wrote his masterpiece for one of the edification of Queen Suryamati, the wife of king Ananth (1028-63).It is based on the *Brihat-katha*, and is written in fiowing narrative style, making delightful reading. It is the largest collection of stories in the world. We Indians of the twentieth and twenty-first-century educated and schooled in the Western type of education have all heard of Hans Christian Anderson and his stories though meant for children make delighfful reading for the adults as well. But Somadeva's contribution made centuries ago did not see the light of the day, due to neglect after the Muslims rule of 500 years. The number of stanzas in his *magnum opus* alone, not counting the prose passages is more than 22,000. It is twice as big as Homer's *Iliad* and the Odyssey put together.

The *Katha-sarita-sagara*, besides being a version of the lost work of Gunadhya, also contains most of the stories contained in the *Panchatantra* This version is quite different from the original and Hertel has advanced a strong case in favour of Kashmir being the original home of *Panchatantra* stories.

It would take an encyclopaedia to list all the writers of folklore ana fables, but it is interesting to note that several anthologies of various topics as love, nature, conduct from the works of eminent Sanskrit poets and authors were compiled in ancient Kashmir. Apart from their value as giving specimen, of some of the best compositions in Sanskrit literature, they provide a clue to the existence of several eminent poets whose works cannot otherwise be traced.

Valabhadeva has compiled *Subhashitavali* containing 3,527 verses in, 101 chapters; they provide a clue to the existence of the several eminent poets whose works cannot otherwise be traced. In addition Shrivara has given us anthologies, which was a cultivated art with Kashmiri literature on the Buddhists religion, law and polity. This was also produced testifying to the versatility of the educated class, who have left their mark on the sands of time.

Chroniclers of the current become historians after a century. Writing about times and life of a society is the base for history. It needs accuracy, economy of words so as not to exaggerate and very objective impartial look at the events of the time. In the field historical compositions, Kashmir perhaps leads and is one of the leaders. The *Nilamat Purana* is a history on pre-historic Kashmir. Kalhana's *Rajatarangini* perhaps the best known historical work on Kashmir occupies a unique position as the only work on history in Sanskrit with a scientific approach of modern historians. Yet Kalhana's pre-historical Kashmir was not the first in this line.

He mentions the work of eleven preceding historians, whose compositions he consulted for producing his famous work. After Kalhana, his tradition and work was continued by others too numerous to name . That the Kashmiri writers possessed a historical sense (a sense of history) is proved by Bilhana's *Vikramadevacharita* which though composed in the *kavya* style was yet superior in historical approach to the works of writers like Bana and Hemachandra.

Today when we look at a society, we give tend to give second place to arts, culture, literature, painting, etc., because the modern god is science and its offspring is technology. Man is rapidly becoming a willing slave of the master called technology, as science fiction has given us a glimpse of the future such as the writings of H.G. Wells and a glimpse of the shape of things to come. It is curious, that we of this century do not look at the scientific achievements of our forefathers.

Medicine is one area, where the modern doctor can still learn not just a thing or two, but a whole lot from literature on the subject left by those who were technologists in one sense. There are original works on medicine from ancient Kashmir. Perhaps as a result of presence of rich flora and fauna in the valley, the *vaidyas* of Kashmir were inspired to conduct research in the science of medicine. Professor

Sylvan Levi after discovering Buddhists manuscripts in Central Asia and China came to the conclusion that the famous Caraka of *charka*, the Author of *Caraka-samhita* was done by Dridhabala, a scholar of Kashmir. Jejjata, the author of the commentary on the *Caraka-samhita* was also a Kashmiri and so was Udbhatta who commented upon *Sushruta-samhita*

Today, there is hardly a teenager who would not have heard of the *Kamasutra*. Whether the young people know or not that Vatsyayana wrote this. It is not material in which century it was written, what is material is that ancient India was also modern. In the area of erotics. Vasunadara whom Kalhana mention as a king ruling in Kashmir after Mihirakula, wrote a book on erotics, *Ratirahasya*, a scientific textbook dealing with the problems of sex, both biological and psychological, written by a Kashmiri *pandit*, the famous Koka, the son of Tejoka. After *Kamasutra* of Vatsyanyana this is a very important though not well-known work on the subject.

11

Manmadhan's Arrows don't Spare Even Kings

His eyes were riveted on the moving figure, the lithesome beauty, who was dancing on the stage. The audience was following every movement she made and the accompanying music was the lullaby that put it together. Several times, he thought she looked at him, and even though him, he stood transfixed to the spot. He was surrounded by his court and officials.

Suddenly he got up. He was the King. The dancers on the stage thought that king did not like the performance, and so there was a hushed silence. The audience craned their necks to see what was happening. The king realised his mistake and shouted.

> Please continue. I got up only to applaud the performance. I am sorry my gesture was misunderstood me. I want to see the rest of the performance.

As he was speaking he saw a pair of eyes from the stage frozen as it were in the *tandava* dance pose, as was her body. Who was she? he wondered . His heart was beating wildly and did not understand what was happening to him. He tried to remind himself: I am the king. I can have anyone I want. But why should a mere dancing girl make my heart flutter?

Meanwhile, the performance continued and eventually ended. Seeing the king's interest in the stage performer, the courtier discreetly found out as to who the dancer was.

Sure enough, as soon as the performance was over, the king

stood from his throne and the artistes were presenter to him one by one. One of them was missing the star.

Where did she go? The silent Question was answered, when she came now dressed differently, bowed before the king in obeisance, till the king bade her stand. They looked at each other. The rest had to follow. Manmadhan never spares any one. His arrows pierced both. Though she tried hard not to show it she was trembling. She knew of love, but never love itself.

Late that night the king went into huddle with his close advisers. He was definitely in love. The adviser saw no problem, the king had a nagging doubt and on that note the meeting ended.

He tried to sleep, but sleep would not come. Her face would come before his eyes and what they said was simply; love. He grew impatient. Why can't the night be over. Exhausted, He fell into a dreamless sleep.

Next morning his favourite courtier entered the room with a sombre expression on his face and the king knew something was wrong.

"Your majesty, the lady who you saw dancing yesterday. It is about her

Yes, yes, what about her?

"She is married ". "What" ?',The anguished cry from the king, who remembered the rule that royalty cannot forcibly take away a man's wife into the royal house.

Who was her husband, was the silent question and the courtier said that he was a rich merchant and a vary pious man.

Then what could be done?

Nothing.

The King was well known for his generosity and his principles. He never broke his own rules, just because he was the king.

He dismissed his courtier and told them not to disturb him.

From that day onwards, the king rarely smiled and busied himself with the affairs of the state. He withdrew himself from the entire merry making in the palace and his queen and wives become anxious about for his health and wellbeing. Soon the news spread in the kingdom. He subjects felt sorry for him and wanted to do something for him but the law was such that it could no broken. Could it be broken? No one knew.

The king used to take long walks in his palace garden and spent his time revising the land revenue rules for the kingdom. He also practised his archery and fighting skills for it was required in those days.

But who was this king is the Question?

He was Pratapaditya II, who ruled Kashmir in the seventh century AD.

12

Will Manmadhan Fail?

SOON, the king got into the habits of sitting alone, reading from the birch-bark writings and writing secretly love poems to his beloved. A chance encounter had changed his life. The courtiers were afraid of approaching him. What would earlier have pleased him? Brought out total indifference to the point of rejection from him. For all practical purposes, he had become ascetic, but how long would it go on. How long would the agony last and drive him insane?

One night, he was resting and gazing at the moon. It was a full moon night and somehow he felt that *chandrama* was trying to communicate with him. Out of the moon's face he saw his beloved smiling at him. In a trance-like state, he continued gazing and in that position fell asleep. . . .

It was she, he was sure. Slowly walking towards him. Am I dreaming, he asked himself. But before he could gather his wits, she was before him kneeling with both hands folded. For a long time, he continued gazing at her fact, so serene, chiseled to the point of a carving, with a hint of the smile that she had given when she was dancing on that fateful night .

My Lord, it was fated that you would come into my life. My mother secretly told me about it, but I laughed at her . When I saw you, my lord, knew the prediction was correct. You see, I had never seen you. Going to open court palace and meeting you were next to impossible and going there with so many people and so many faces was not proper. He nodded dumb at the apparition before him, wearing the same *sari* that she wore on that day. He would give up anything for her sake.

She continued:

> When I was fourteen, I was married. I had not even seen that man, I married, but had to obey my parents. He is a good man and encouraged me to learn dancing and music. I play the *veena* too.

As she said this, a shy smile and the hint of the dimple on her cheek appeared. He wanted touch her, but that was not to be, even in dreams.

> From my previous *karma*, I knew who my lord was, but could not do anything about it. My heart is crying for you, my soul moans for you. You are the *maharaja* and salvation lies in your hand. Please take care of yourself, don't worry about me I shall pray for your health and safety.

He wanted to say something, but no words would come. He pinched himself, not yet awake.

Hours later, the sun's rays on his face coming through a gap in the curtain woke him up. For a while, he did not know where he was and then with a jerk, he remembered everything.

That day the courtiers were amazed at the transformation in the king. He laughed for first time in the months. He ate well, talked to his queens and even played with the children of his relatives.

He looked forward to the night, when he hoped she would come again. So far, even he did not know her name, but a courtier by accident dropped her name while discussing about her husband.

She was Damayanti. What a beautiful name.

She never came back in his dreams, but he kept hoping. Then one day the court astrologer came accompanied by his dewans.

"Your Majesty, we have come to talk about a very confidential matter with you."

He nodded and then they proceeded to tell him what lay in the store for him. The astrologer said: "we will have a queen who will be a commoner, but you will marry her."

"Yes, but how?"

"She has of her own accord, started dancing in the Shiva temple at Avantipura (a town about 35 km from Srinagar). You know what that means."

What does that mean he asked totally mystified..

"It means you can marry her."

"How?"

"You can accept her from a temple as a dancing girl put there by her husband on account of her skill in dancing. He was not forced and she belongs to the temple. He will not have any objection as per our *parampara*."

He looked doubtful, but they persuaded him to accompany them to Avantipura and see for himself.

Though he was disgi iised her piercing beautiful eyes sought him out of hundreds who were watching the performance. His heart was full of joy at seeing her.

Soon a courtier went to see the temple priest and the husband was sent for. Since he had sent her to the temple of his own accord and she wanted to leave he said, "If she is happy to go with another man and live with him, I have no objection". The king was silently watching the dialogue from a corner and when heard this, his heart leapt with joy.

Within an hour, the marriages rites performed in the temple itself and the king Pratapaditya who had come empty handed from the palace returned with his beloved.

So, after all the agony, ecstasy followed.

Manmadhan did not fail and the Kashmir king consummated his love.

13

Fine Arts Need no Frontiers

FINE arts, by its very definition, cannot be cultivated in a day. It is a combination of skills, dedication, consistency, quality and tradition that builds it up. Kashmir too had its fine arts with its ancient tradition. Excavations at Harwan near Srinagar depicts a dancer in a pose and other sites show a female musician playing on a *dholak*. There are several references to dance, drama and music in the *Rajatarangini*. It was in the seventh and eighth centuries AD that these arts reached the pinnacle of their glory. In fact, no student of classicai Indian dances can ignore or bypass the commentaries on Bharata's *Natya- Shastra* and the original works on dances like those of authors like Udbhatta, Lollapata, Sankuka, Bhattanayaka and the last but the greatest of them all, Abhinavagupta. The *tandava* dance of Shiva is described in *Harvijayakavya* by Rajakaratnakara.

In the twentieth century, when we think of classical dance form, we always think of the Bharatanatyam, Kathak, Mohiniattam, Oddissi, Kathakkali, Manipuri. One would notice that they do span a large portion of the country territorially, but are appreciated by the people universally. However, the Kashmir dance form has been unfortunately lost in antiquity. While the finer traditions in the music and dance have been preserved in the rest of India by the hereditary professionals artistes, who passed them on from generation to generation, in the case of Kashmir especially after the eleventh century AD there were only civil wars, invasions, repression, blood shed, in the name of conquest and religious bigotry.

But a look at what little was preserved at least in books. As elsewhere in India, classical dancing in Kashmir also had a religious background, the temple being the centre of all activity including cultural and educational. The first references to dancing in *Rajatarangini* is about king Jalauka, the son of successor of Emperor Ashoka, who was an ardent worshipper of Shiva and a lover of music and dance.

While worshiping at the shrine of Shiva, "a hundred among the ladies who had risen to dance in honour of the god at the time fixed for dancing and singing he gave out of joy to *jyestnarudra*". Dancing in temples as the most authoritative chronicle of the time *Rajatarangini* says, was a hereditary calling with certain families. Temple dancing as the *devadasi* system has shown fell into disrepute due abuses, but in ancient India temple dancers had an honoured place in society as in the Gupta period, women occupied honourable positions in the professions as well. They were not the tagged appendages to men as happened in later centuries, but people in their own right who out of choice danced in a temple. It was no slur either on her or her family. Sadly, while the system totally disappeared in Kashmir, in the rest of the country, wherever it flourished it degenerated into prostitution.

Lalitaditya (AD 724-61) perhaps the most famous in ancient Kashmir, was a king who believed in innovation and was open to conviction. Once outhunting in the jungle, he came across two beautiful damsels dancing gracefully to the accompaniment of a drum. He asked them as to why they were dancing in the jungle. Pat came the reply; We come from a family ol professional dancers and we live in the village yonder. By the direction of our mothers, who got their living here, we perform at this spot.

This custom handed down by tradition, has become fixed in our family. Although surprised, Lalitaditya began to think. If there was a tradition there was bound to be some proof. He consulted his builder and the master builder of the kingdom (in those days engineers were called builders and the word went from India to ancient Egypt as well). The site where Lalitaditya found the girls dancing was excavated and to his amazement, he found a large temple containing two beautiful images of Shiva and Vishnu, which he installed in two temples in his new city of Parihasupura.

That this profession was not looked down upon is apparent from another passage in *Rajatarangini* where in it is mentioned that the king Chakravarman married two professional dancers sisters Hamsi and Nagalatha and although they belonged to a lower caste, he made Hamsi his first queen, who enjoyed among the king's wives the privileges of being fanned with the choweries — a kind of fan made of exquisite material.

A look at the sculptures and relief on the walls of the old temple reveals figures of dancers with ornament and graceful styles of hair dressing. It appears that classical (Indian dancing as systematised by Bharat was in vogue in Kashmir). It was, however, in the eleventh century AD that King Zain-ul-abuddin from the pen of shrivara. There is also a reference to the *tandava* dance of Shiva in several verses of *Rajatarangini*. The *tandava* dance represents the five activities (*panchakarya*). — That is CREATION, PRESERVATION, INCARNATION, DESTRUCTION AND DELIVERANCE.

Thus, dance did flourish in ancient Kashmir, but it was lost under the jack boots of tyranny that destroyed a civilisation. But dance is always accompanied by music and drama is but a cousin for the spoken word and needs to be heard if not face to face, at least on the stage. But more of that later.

14

If Music be the Food of Love, Then Play on

WHEN we think of music in the Indian sense of the term, we don't think of Michael Jackson or Mike Jagger or Apache Indian. We think in terms of schools of music. Carnatic music to us means a serious way of life. The performer performs whether it is Hindustani music, light classical or semi-classical. Music is an accompaniment, the yearning to express something beautifully and delicately punctuated by sounds that get glorified by the way they are played on the instruments.

And Shakespeare was not far wrong when the said: " If music be the food of love, then play on".

Did Kashmir have its own music and if so, why have we not heard of it till now?

Yes, ancient Kashmir did have it, but it was destroyed as a science by the ravages of time and the savagery of man.

Today, we talk of socialism although the high priest of it would have been horrified to see the end result of it. For Karl Marx, the biggest obsession was what he perceived as exploitation and its end to bring man and man on an equal level. But look at music and its history. It was patronised by those who could afford it and in that age it was the kings and the *rajas*. Even the audience had to be what we today call educated enough in the fine arts to appreciate the finer points of the art.

Strangely enough, a voluntary kind of socialism prevailed in ancient Kashmir, when the king and the commoner together cultivated music by patronising it and participating in it. The *Rajatarangini*, the most authoritative history of Kashmir, supplies certain vital clues about the development of music in ancient Kashmir. Music was played, we are told, in Buddhist *viharas* during the reign of Jaluka, son of Ashoka. The king was himself a lover of music and maintained a troupe of dancing girls and musicians. At the Hindu sacred shrines and in temples, "Music was played to the accompaniment of big drums, cymbals, etc. At several religious ceremonies, particularly connected with the tantric worship music was a must." says PNK Bamzai, the most authoritative historian of Kashmir of modern times. Mamma, a blind musician was, for example, specially employed to play at the time of tantric worship.

We talk of society and do differentiate naturally between the rich and the poor. What a rich man can afford becomes a profession for the poor. Ib you want lullabys to be sung, apart from your mother, none will oblige but the rich, the nobility of Kashmir, not to forget the kings, all had such tastes, call it weakness for the lullaby. What the walkman, or the stereo music of today or the visual of television can do, the ancient musicians did by singing to their masters (or customers in modern parlance) to induce sleep. The ancient kings of Kashmir invariably listened to songs and the music of the flute and the flute at bedtime. Some of them were great adept in this art. Kings created a taste among the Kashmiris for light opera songs (*upanga-gita*), Harsha, amusing his father in public with songs, as if he were a singer, kept up his establishment with the presents the former gave him. He also gave music lessons to several courtiers among whom was Kanaka, the uncle of the famous historian Kalhana. He was a great patron of music. He presented to a musician named Bhimanayaka, an elephant together with a female elephant, when he gave an outstanding performance.

Since computers had not been invented with memory then, records are sketchy, but we do get a glimpse though the time span is obviously different. The professional musician has been described as being addicted to keeping late hours, eating much meat and drinking incessantly. This quotation is from *Rajatarangini*, but in sequence it was much later, than the period we are describing. However, keeping in view today's standards, one would venture to say, that

skilful delineator of the gods born in Marwar (modern Rajastan) named Sringadhara: he left behind his paintings and other masterpieces like those produced by yakshas. Those who followed his lead were called 'the old Western School'.

After describing the extension of the influence of the Western School on Bengal, Bihar, Orissa and Nepal, Taranath proceeds to talk about the Kashmir School.

> In Kashmir, too, there were in former times followers of the old Western school of Madhyadesa, later on a certain Hasuraya founded a new school of painting and sculpture, which is called the Kashmir School.

Being the home of Mahayana Buddhism, Kashmiri painters and sculptors carried their art tradition even further north, to Central Asia and China. The aim of the Buddhist artist was to visualise the ideals of his creed: to illustrate by pictorial parables of all the beautiful sentiments of his religion. These were designed to appeal to the higher feelings of the spectator. What political upheavals and natural calamities destroyed in Kashmir, remains preserved in the caves and cities buried in the soil of Central Asia.

"Kashmir murals", writes Dr. Goetz, an authority on the subject, "we know only from places outside the valley. The earlier style in the part of the Gandharan murals at Ming-Oil (Kucha) in the northern Tarim Basin, the latter, in the frescoes of Man-nan and of the "Red temple at Tsaparang in Western Tibet; and illustrated manuscripts have turned up in Tibet. The style of the school of Hasuraya has more vitality than the Bengal miniatures, but harde line and brighter, but rather cold colours"

Early artiste in ancient Kashmir fused a specially processed ground on cloth to paint on. A specimen of this is the remarkable set of twenty-four large paintings on cotton preserved in the Victoria and Albert Museum, London, which though painted in the middle of sixteenth century, yet shows the material that the early painters had at their disposal. The colours were all vegetables and mineral, which lasted longer and also produced a better effect.

Kashmiris were adept at painting designs on dress material, which looked so real that when King Harsha's palace was looted after his defeat at the hands of rebel forces, some looters eager to get gold, burned clothes which were painted with gold, and then anxiously searched the ashes.

So ends the tale of painting . . . today also there is a distinct school, but that is the modern age.

16

Etched in Stone, they sing silently

"OF all the arts" observes the famous British expert Percy Brown practised by the people of the Kashmir valley, in the pre-Islamic period, building construction was one in which they were notably proficient, as the remains of their large monuments in stone are a standing proof. His account in 'Indian Architecture' describes the various schools of architecture from ancient times and rate the Kashmir contribution highly.

Though time may have robbed the specimen of such magnificent architecture of its fullness, having to brave the ravages of time and predators mostly, two legged, the style, which culminated in such masterpieces of architecture as Martand and Avantipura, must have had a long history of development. That it was a product of blending of influences from different classical schools is evident from the trefoil and the horse-shoe arches and from the fluted pillars. Archaeologists have been attempting to line the beginning of architectural trends in Kashmir to the Buddhist *stupas* and *caitya*, foundations, some of which were recently excavated at Harwan and Ushkur. However, due to lack of exact data available, it is not quite clear as to whether there is really a link between the two. Further, Kalhana has made references to foundations made by Kings and queens long before the date of Harwan and Ushkur (third -fourth century AD).

Kalhana's *Rajatarangini* has clearly mentioned that Emperor Ashoka founded the city of Srinagar and also a Buddhist settlement in the valley at Sukseletra. But it is not the Srinagar of today. No traces of Ashoka's city are now left, but we do have an authoritative account of its grandeur by the famous Chinese traveller of the time

Heun-Tsiang, who refers to it as the 'Old Capital'.

Stone architecture was much older than what Kalhana has mentioned or as described by Heun-Tsiang. There is a gap of several centuries, which scholars to this day are trying to bridge waiting for more excavations to pinpoint definitely and prove that Harwan and Ushkur were specimens of Buddhist settlements of later period. When Gandhara having lost much of its importance as a stronghold of Buddhism no longer appealed to monks and preachers, who migrated in numbers to more hospitable land of Kashmir. Thus, Harwan and Ushkur proves Greek, Roman and Byzantine influence on the development of architecture in the Kashmir valley.

One hears of Arya or Aryan, but even today there is some difference of opinion about its origin. But be that as it may, it is the stone architecture of Kashmir temples dotting the valley that attracts the expert, the archaeologist and the lay tourist.

Cunningham was the first expert do an on the spot study of the ruins of the temples in the valley, and it was he, who calls their style of architecture, the 'Aryan Order'. This name is appropriate, for it merits the title as there is a distinct identity that this type of architecture has.

What distinguishes the Kashmiri or Kashmirian architecture, from others is items like lofty pyramidal roofs, its treoiled doorways, covered by pyramidal pediments and the great width of its inter columnations. That it was influenced by Greek and Roman styles from the Indo-Greeks during the time of their control over the Kabul valley (Afghanistan) and western Punjab.

The fame of Kashmiri architecture had spread far and wide, for one of the names for the people of the valley was 'Shastra-Silpina' or architects, a term which could only have been applied to them on account of their skill in building. One wonders how in those ancient days massive stones were lifted and laid in position with great precision on the heights of the Kashmiri temples. But Kashmiris did know the science and laws of mechanics, then, as they sent *yantras* or machines in lifting up enormously bulky and heavy stones.

Perhaps the earliest specimen of this order of architecture is the temple on the Shankaracharya hill; the ruins at Loduv and the Pravaresa temple at the foot of the Hari Parbat hill.

The real patron and to some extent the founder of the sophisticated Aryan style of Kashmir architecture was Lalitaditya the king, who built the city of Parihaspura with its imposing temples and caityas, the famous Sun temple. In his constructions, we see a transformation achieved by the absorption of many new ideas and techniques from the rest of India and counties to the north of Kashmir and to the west. Like many empire builders, Lalitaditya took artistes from wherever he could obtain them and tried to mould different styles and techniques into a new imperial art bearing the impress of his own royal personality.

King Lalitaditya's principal minister, Cankuna, was a former Chinese official, who erected the great stupa at parihaspura and other stupas at Pandrentan, decorated with sculptures in the Y and the T Chinese art.

The great caitya of his of which the foundations have been unearthed follows the Gandhara style of architecture in his plan and Kalhana records the installation in it of a huge Buddha image, modelled perhaps on the Bamiyan Colossus in modern Afghanistan.

Such is the story of stones and their makers. What they made is still there braving the ravages of time, but standing there as mute witnesses to its passage and proclaiming their identity to elements and the humans who take care to look at them and understand them.

17

The Arrow that Boomeranged

THE swish of water was discernible as twenty-four arms pulled the oars of the royal barge down the Vitasta. Sitting in middle with luxurious trappings absolute power was the King of Kashmir.

It was summer, and the gentle breeze hit his face, as he sat contented, or so it seemed. But he was bored, a king without troubles, yet with much to worry about. On the banks of the river, as his barge sailed by, people bowed to their king.

As the royal barge was nearing Chattabal, where the river branches off toward Shadipur, he saw on the bank, a Kashmiri *pandit* girl. The king had given orders for distinctive dresses to be worn by his Hindu and Muslim subjects. It was the dress that identified the girl who was about 15 years of age and was filling an earthen pot with water, unaware that the King was looking at her. Suddenly, the King got the urge to do something if only to prove that he was a warrior as well.

On an impulse, he picked up his bow and fitted an arrow, which he aimed at the girl. But the girl was not the target. The earthen pot on her head was. He arched back and the arrow flew out half across the Vitasta, and hit the pot. Expecting water to spurt out, the King looked at the girl, who had her back turned towards him.

The parts of the earthen pot fell from her head, but lo and behold, the water did not. It stayed as if stuck by gum to her head, keeping the rounded shape of the earthern pot intact. She slowly turned around, calmly looking at the King and expressed her anger by cursing him, thus:

> Puynaye mound, Zuu sel naye myni phulhare seeth.
>
> May you get the disease and may the cure lie in my footwear (sandal worn by Kashmiris made of grass)

Soon enough, the King fell ill and the disease was diagnosed as incurable. The doctors, were puzzled as no cure was found to be effective.

Eminent physicians of that time were consulted, but to no avail. The King was asked about his illness. But no solution was found.

Lying on his bed in his palace, he idly thought about the innocuous things and tried to recall whether he had done anything to invite a curse or black-magic on himself. Suddenly, there flashed through his mind the picture of the girl with the earthen pot. Maybe, she cursed me for breaking her water pot. The more he thought about it, the more he was convinced that the key to his disease lay with the Kashmiri *pandit* girl.

He summoned his Wazir and told him about the incident. The Wazir thought for a while and said,

> Your Highness, it is well nigh impossible to trace a girl in this city of Srinagar where over a lakh of inhabitants live. And you have seen her from a distance.
>
> But, I shall try to think of a way of tracing her. If her curse is the cause, she must be someone unusual. Maybe the neighbours in her mohalla would know about her powers. Maybe, we can after all do something about curing your illness.

So, teams of people were sent out to locate the young girl, who unfortunately for posterity shall remain nameless, in the city of Srinagar. Eventually, they found her and begged her to restore the King to health. They asked her forgiveness on behalf of the King and promised untold wealth and riches to her.

She was annoyed and expressed it in no uncertain terms:

> Has all the gold and wealth that he has helped him cure his illness. Don't talk about money, foolish men.

And dismissing them, she said:

> here, take ma pulhoru (grass sandal) and burn it. Take the ash and smear it on your Sultan's body. He will recover.

And with that she dismissed them, the courtiers, overjoyed, rushed back to the palace to burn the grass sandal and use the ashes to cure the King.

A Brahman, ascetic named Shree Bhat was a contemporary of the King. He watched the developments and knew through his inner sight thal the King would recover, but how to take out the thoughts of revenge from his mind. Being a realised soul, he travelled by foot to the Parimahal caves on the banks of the Dal Lake and stayed in a cave nearby.

Legend has it that he left his body there, the mortal remains remaining hidden, from view and his soul flew to the palace and as the King still on his death-bed was struggling, entered his body. Recovery was fast and dramatic and it was after this incident that the King ushered in an era of peace and prosperity in Kashmir, for which he became famous in posterity and today, his is perhaps the only reign that is remembered for its benign rule and prosperity and peace that followed.

Shiva

18

A Wedding at Mount Kailash

LORD Shiva was in a pensive mood. Gods have goddesses as their consorts but he had none. It was of course ordained by divine grace that Parvati should be his consort. And time too was decided earlier. It had yet to come. Meanwhile, after *tapasya*, on Mount Kailash, the snow capped, peak, the Lord was in a pensive mood when he heard 'Narayana, Narayana, Narayana . . . ', the chant preceded the arrival of Narada, his devoted disciple.

Lord, the time has come for us to make preparations for your wedding I have already been to Goddess Parvati's parent's house and preparations have already started there. On the bridegroom's side, it is my responsibility to make the preparations. The bridegroom has to be clothed in proper attire and the *barat* has to be organised (*barat* is the bridegroom's party that accompanies him to the bride's house). Also we have to organise proper transportation.

Lord Shiva closed his eyes and did not respond. After a while Narada took the hint and left. Days passed.

The wedding had been fixed for trayodashi (thirteenth day from the full moon night) of the month of Phalguna, when in the Himalayas, the intensity of cold lessens and points to the coming of the spring. As the date was already known, it became a topic of conversation among the gods and goddesses. Parvati had many visitors and among them were her friends too, while none dared to go to Mount Kailash to congratulate the bridegroom.

Came the wedding day and Narada was everywhere directing, suggesting and even shouting about arrangements. But everything came to nought with the Lord refusing to wear any earthly clothes. He had covered himself with the basam from the *shimshan ghat* and the only order he gave to Narada was to give a bath to Nandikeshvara (in Kashmir he is known by his Sanskrit name, Vrishabha), the holy bull on whose back, the Lord would ride quite often.

The *lagna* or the auspicious time to tie the knot was fixed for midnight as per the celestial direction. Thus, just an hour before midnight when all preparations were finished, the Lord said, he did not want any *barat*. Only Vrishaba and Narada were to accompany him. And strangely enough, though Narada had issued so many invitations, none turned up. He was mystified and wondered, whether the Lord had a hand in it.

One extremely important thing worried Narada: Custom and tradition dictates that the bridegroom carry presents for his bride and give them to her before the wedding ceremony. Narada could not summon the courage to broach the subject. But he felt that though he might be chastised, he should remind the Lord about it. Maybe, he forgot.

> Lord, we should carry a present for the bride, an ornament, or jewel or clothes. I don't know....

For the first time, Lord Shiva opened his eyes and looked at Narada "I have already made arrangements, you don't have to worry about it."

"But we have to wrap it and prepare . . ."

"Enough, I told you I have already made arrangements . . ."

In the corner, Vrishabha was munching on a fresh supply of grass totally content, and looking fresh and shining against the backdrop of Mount Kailash. And so the wedding procession started with Narada in tow following on foot.

But having a nagging doubt about the present, of which he did not see any sign. And on this auspicious occasion, he did not want to annoy the Lord, whose wrath on this day he did not want to incur.

Parvati

It was almost near the midnight hour. About half a *kos* (a *kos* was a measure of distance in ancient times measuring about two miles of today), away from the bride's house it started snowing. Or so it seemed to Narada, who did not pay any attention to it, shivering as he was walking blehind the bridegroom.

As they reached the door of the bride's house, Lord Shiva turned round and looked at Narada and said:

"Is that present enough?"

Narada was stupefied for a second and suddenly realised while shaking the snow flakes from his shoulders, that his Lord, was making fun of him:

Yes, my lord it is appropriate also.

And so they went into Goddess Parvati's house and the wedding was solemnised with all the Gods and Goddess watching from the heavens.

The rest as all of us know is history. But what was so special about the snow flakes that Lord Shiva talked about?

It was not snow flakes but flakes of gold dust that surrounded as they fell from the heavens, the entire village where Parvati and her parents lived, a fitting present for the Lord's bride, the future mother of Lord Ganesha ana Lord Muruga.

And that is the day the midnight hour when *Shivaratri* is celebrated from Kashmir to Kanya-Kumari or frorn Rajkot to Arunachal Pradesh since the last ten thousand years of *kali-yuga*.

And to this day it snows on that night, there is thunder lightning rain and on the upper reaches of the Himalayas where Lord Shiva has his abode Mount Kailash it certainly snows there.

Unbelievable to believe that *Shivaratri* celebrated for thousands of years in February should be celebrated in June. Yet it is the belief and faith that illustrates the way of life of the Kashmiri Hindu that faith can conquer even time and space.

Jabbar Khan was an Afghan, the younger brother of Sardar Azim Khan, the Afghan Governor appointed by Kabul to rule over

Kashmir in the eighteenth century. After Islam had come to Kashmir (Islam carne to Kashmir in 1338) when his elder brother left for Kandahar (modern Afghanistan) Jabbar Khan was in charge of Kashmir.

Jabbar Khan was once told by someone that it was a comrnon notion among Kashrniri Hindus that snow would invariably fall or there would be sleet or storm or heavy rain on *Shivaratri* night (thirteenth night of the dark fortnight ot Phalguna). He was intrigued.

To test this he ordered that all the Hindus in the valley would not be allowed to observe this festival in Phalguna (February), but in Har (June) which is summer. Accordingly, it had to be observed on the corresponding night in the latter month.

But it seemed unthinkable, since June is a summer month. A conclave of all the wise man of the community decided to accept the challenge and as Pandit Anand Koul says in his treatise on the community published in 1924. They summoned all their spirituai powers as devotees of Lord Shiva to accomplish this impossible task.

Came the night and Jabbar Khan was watching from the balcony at Shergarhi (a locality of Srinagar) of his palace. It was an hour before midnight. The sky was clear, not a cloud in sight. Knowing he had won against the non-believer, Jabbar Khan decided to go to bed.

An hour later past the hour of midnight, Jabbar Khan was woken up from his sleep, as winds and rain lashed that palace. He rushed out, calling up his guards and looked up at the sky. It was dark, with clouds and as he stepped out, snowflakes followed the rainfall and brought the temperature down considerably.

A thoroughly humiliated Jabbar Khan went back to the palace. But the bard, who witnessed it, mocked him by saying:

> Look at Jabbar, the wretch. Even Har (June) has turned into winter.

Such was Kashmir then.

Narad

19

Narada — Scribe Extraordinary

IN the Hindu folklore, Narada has been the wandering bard, the sage, the advisor and most important of all the observer for Lord Shiva of what was and is happening in this world. In other words reporter at large.

This has been aptly described by Shri K.K. Nair (Edit Page, *Times of India*, dated 4th October, 1999):

Narada, the divine sage, is the most colourful figure in the Hindu religious literature. He is one of the sons of Brahma. Possessed of sacred learning and noble conduct, this all-knowing wandering saint who is highly intelligent and tactful is respected by gods as well as demons.

Procrastination is unknown to Narada. If an issue crops, he applies his mind, tries to find a solution himself and if he fails, he rushes to his father Brahma, Lord Narayana or Lord Shiva and ensures that evil forces are destroyed. The general feeling about Narada is that he likes to generate quarrels. This is a mistake. Narada does everything for the general good.

One who never finds happiness when others are in trouble, Narada uses his mystery of the art of reconciliation through his powers of speech and deep wisdom. He hates no one. That Narada is one of the wisest sages is borne out by the fact that it was on his advice Sage Vaimiki, the first poet, composed the *Ramayana* and Veda-Vyasa composed *Bhagavata*.

Singing praises of Lord Narayana, Narada used to be welcomed by all. As one who was very close to Lord Narayana, sometimes

Narada used to be caught in the web of ego. He felt that he was the greatest devotee of the Lord. This ego of Narada was tackled by the Lord more than once to drive home the truth that there were others who were equally devoted to the Lord, some even scoring better than the divine saint.

Once Narada went to Dvaraka and found that Lord Narayana was rolling on the ground with a splitting headache. All medicines proved' ineffective. Narada was obviously upset and asked the lord, 'Is there no medicine for this?'. The Lord told him that 'there was a medicine but it was very difficult to get'. Narada offered to go to any lengths so that the suffering of the Lord could be ended. 'A handful of dust from the feet of any devotees can help me', The Lord said. Narada thought why can't he give the dust himself. But he thought it to be sin to smear the Lord's forehead with the dust from his feet. Similarly, Narada's efforts to get the dust were in vain as no one was ready to commit such a sin.

Crestfallen, Narada went back to the Lord and asked him to suggest a way of getting the dust. The lord told him to go to Brindavan where the *gopikas* lived. Narada was surprised. What do they know about *bhakti*, he thought. Yet, he went there and the distressed *gopikas* gave enough dust to Narada and forced him to rush it to the Lord.

When Narada came with the dust, the Lord was sitting and laughing. His headache had gone. He told Narada,

> You consider yourself as the greatest of my devotees but you were not ready to put an end to my suffering. You thought of committing a sin by giving dust from your feet. But the *gopikas* never thought of this. For them ending my pain was important. And the thought of any sin did not occur them. So who is the greatest devotee?

Narada's inflated ego thus got a jolt.

On another occasion, Narada boasted before the Lord that no devotee could equal him. This time, the lord spoke of a farmer as one of his greatest devotees and asked Narada to see him to convince himself. Humiliated and upset, Narada went to the village where he saw the farmer immersed in his work from dawn to dusk, rearing his cattle, ploughing the fields, etc. During this time he uttered the name of the Lord thrice — once when he woke up, once before taking his midday food and once before retiring to bed, whereas Narada was going round singing melodious songs in the praise of the Lord.

He rushed to the Lord and asked how this farmer could be rated as one of the greatest devotees. Laughing at Narada's plight, the Lord gave him a vessel of water, which was full to the brim and asked Narada to go round and round. After sometime, he asked Narada to stop and the Lord asked him how may times he had thought of the Lord. As Narada was concentrating entirely on not spilling the water, he forgot all about the Lord. He had to admit his lapse.

The Lord told Narada,

> You forgot me completely while doing this small job. In contrast, the farmer does physical labour the whole day without any rest, yet he has time to think of me at least thrice. So is not the farmer a greater devotee?

Narada was humbled.

The lesson is that remembering the name of God even once a day with devotion is much more beneficial than giving lip service to religion and spirituality.

Measuring devotion

Shiva and Parvati were sitting on Mount Kailash and looking down at the world of mortals. Suddenly, Parvati posed a question to her Lord: 'Who do you think among the mortals is your greatest devotee?' Lord Shiva was silent for a while looking at the vast expense of a white carpet that was snow on the slope leading to mount Kailash.

"I do not know, but I suppose we could find out."

At this moment, Narada, his able assistant and journalist extraordinary came in chanting 'Narayan, Narayan'.

Ganesh

Meanwhile, Parvati said: "what about that man, who is doing penance with his legs tied up on the tree and his face and eyes getting smoke from the ground holy fire.

With his *trikaladrishti*, Lord Shiva saw his devotee doing exactly what Parvati said.

"Why do not you give the poor man your *darshana*. He has been doing *tapasya* for the last 14 years.

"All right, we shall settle it finally."

Lord Shiva called Narada and gave his new field assignment, "Go down into the mortal world and find out who is my true *bhakta* (devotee)?. Remember the man has been doing *tapasya* for the last 14 years. Check on him". As Narada turned to go, Lord Shiva called after him. "Narada, there is also a *chursi* (opium addict), who is also a devotee of mine. Find out if he needs anything and ask him this question, "Can an elephant pass through the eye of a needle? Ask the *tapasvi* the same question and tell me what he says."

Within minutes, Narada with his dress changed, was winging his way down to Bharat.

As he was walking, chanting Narayan, Narayan, he came upon a big tree and saw the devotee who had doing *tapasya* for 14 years. He wished him and asked him as to what he was doing and if he needed anything?

"Are you blind. I am getting blind. I am doing *tapasya* since 14 years and waiting for Lord Shiva to give me *darsana*."

"I am sorry to disturb you, but now that I am here, could you answer a small question for me."

The man gave an irritated sigh and asked, "What is your question?"

"Can an elephant pass through the eye of a needle?"

"Are you mad. How can an elephant pass through the eye of a

needle. Go away and leave me in peace."

Narada walked away and as he left the forest, he saw a hut with some smoke coming out of it. He called out, 'anybody home?' No answer. He pushed the door open and found inside a man siting under a torn quilt. He was shivering, but he got up and welcomed Narada. And Narada asked, whether he needed anything?

"No, I do not need any riches. But I would like to have a new quilt and a little opium. My Lord Shiva has taken care of me and I am sure, he will take care of me."

Narada's mind went back to Lord Shiva's instructions and resolved to help this poor shlvenng man.

"You do not worry, I shall take care of it, but before I go, can you answer a question."

"Can an elephant pass through the eye of a needle?"

"Yes, if the Lord wishes it so."

"Thank you", said Narada.

And so, the roving Narada winged his way to Mount Kailash to make his report. After he finished giving the details of his encounter with the two mortals, Lord Shiva turned with a smile to Parvati:

"You see, my real *bhakta* is the *chursi* and not the other man who is doing *tapasya* for 14 years.

Moral : *Faith can move mountains*
Faith embodies devotion.
Faith is the inner strength.
Faith has no ego.
Faith is the ultimate step towards moksha.

20

Rationalising the Rituals

VARANASI, on the banks of the Mighty Ganga. The chief *munni* had called for a meeting for he had been troubled for long at the battering that Hindu *dharma* was taking at the hands of the *mlechchhas* all over Bharat. Something had to be done. Movement had become now a part of life and with that the concept of the *gotra* was and its application to rituals in daily life were becoming difficult.

Time had become short, distances long, and separation of families the order of the day. Some kind of reformation was necessary. Simplification was the need of the hour, the day and the age. So, with all the *pandits* around him, he explained his idea. There was instant opposition to it. But being wise in the ways of the world, the chief *muni*, started a discussion pointing out the practical difficulties of rituals the Brahmanical order had prescribed from birth to death and even thereafter for the Hindu.

The discussion continued for seventeen days. At the end, there was a compromise. That certain ceremonies should be curtailed, at birth, at marriage and after death. With these three it was decided to begin, the process of reformation. But being Hindu and being open to conviction in changing times, it was also decided that views of others from all parts of Bharat should also be ascertained, before finally bringing about the change.

There is rigidity in formalised religion; there is a set of do's and don'ts, but there is no deviation, but for tile Hindu the path is not one, but many that he can tread. Today as we are ready for walking on the bridge year 2000 in preparation for stepping into the new century and the millennium, we are told that Democracy in India came from Westminster, but look at the practice of discussion on philosophy and religion that has been a hallmark of the Hindu faith. The fact that the Varanasi *pandits* wanted to hear the views of others in the faith points to the undeniable fact that inner democracy was very much evident in India, long before the first European came ashore.

A Mahasammelan was planned a year hence and arrangements were made to inform all the religious leaders in every corner of India. From Dvaraka in the west to Assam in the east and from Varanasi to Magadh and down south to Kanyakumari emissaries were sent. Up north to Kashmir also the news had to be conveyed. As is well known today, so also then, each area or region had its religious head. He had to be informed. He could himself come, or due to an exigency, send his representative.

Lovgakshi Muni was the chief *muni* of Kashmir, *rishi* of outstanding qualities, whose fame had spread far and wide. Wise and well read, he was a scholar of eminence, a debator on philosophy and metaphysics and his attendance was essential at the Varanasi Mahasammelan. It was Magh (January) and the messenger crossed along with his party the Chenab river in Punjab and moved on towards Kashmir.

Alas, the mighty Himalaya was snow bound, the passes through the mountains were blocked for the next three months and had been so since the previous two months. They decided to return to Varanasi and report failure to inform Lovgakshi Muni about the Mahasammelan.

And so when the *sammelan* began in Varanasi, the whole of Bharat was represented except Kashmir. The *sammelan* lasted several months and decisions of far-reaching consequences were taken. While the rest of the representatives returned to their respective areas, with the new reformed list of rituals, Kashmir remained in the dark.

And to this day, the rituals of the Kashmiri Hindus are the most complicated, though a practical effort is on to trim the rituals in preparation for the coming twenty-first century.

21

The Thread that Joins us Together

INDIA, wrote Jawahar lal Nehru in 1937, is a bundle of contradictions held together by an invisible thread. Indian civilisation used to be called the Hindu civilisation, but having been Anglicised (Nehru included) it became in the English language the Indian civilisation — the idea being to identify the people not by their faith or way of life, but by geography. We, the modern generation of Indians especially those professing the Hindu faith take festivals for granted. Time was a decade or two ago, when the suited booted sahib would barely tolerate the tradition, suffering it in disdainful silence. But times have changed and the Indian of today is fast searching for his roots and proud of it.

Festivals in ancient India, united the country — not politically as we understand it today, but socially and spiritually. Almost all our festivals have a scientific basis, which the modern Indian understands after going all the way to Harvard or Cambridge or Heidelberg universities. The West has suddenly discovered that *Ayurveda* is a science of healing, which the Englishman of Kipling's generation dismissed as native quackery.

There was this young man the first one in his village to go abroad, study and work there. After years, he came back home for a visit. The entire village turned out to welcome him. After the initial euphoria of relatives flocking and presents being distributed, there was a lull. And during the exchanging of views and greetings and gifts, his old grandfather was totally ignored, sitting in one corner watching the proceedings.

Suddenly, the young man realised his mistake and sat down with his grandpa who casually asked him:

"What work do you do?"

"Grandpa, I am a futurologist. I work. . . ."

"What is that?"

"Essentially, it is forecasting based on various hypothesis availabie to provide a guideline for the future. Like telling what will happen five years hence."

Baring a toothless smile, grandpa beamed and said:

"I understand now perfectly... you know" he bent down and whispered:

"We also had this in our country....ø

"We did?"

"Yes, it was called astrology."

Crestfallen, the young man realised what he had already heard in the US, that everything in this country was not superstition, but it had elements of knowledge in it.

And so it is with festivals. They have a purpose. It has now been proved beyond doubt that the movement of the sun and the moon do effect human behaviour and other physical phenomena such as tides, climate, etc., however, due to the Western influence we have tended to underrate their importance.

Talking of festivals, from Kashmir to Kanyakumari and Rajkot to Arunachal Pradesh, *Shivaratri* is celebrated. The language is different, the ingredients used for the *puja* may be varied, but the thread of similarity is there. Take *Deepavali* as it is called in the south. In the north it is called *Diwali*, Festival of Lights no dispute about that. In the north, they prepare sweets for the children and serve them on dried leaves. In the south, the same is served on plantain leaf. The social theme, when it gains acceptance gets absorbed into what is deemed to be a religious practice.

After all, the temple has been the centre for running the social, cultural, educational aspects of daily life. Even the villaye *pahalvan* or wrestler was meant for the initial defence of the weak and the meek. The army of the king came later. We poke fun when someone observes *Amavasya* and Purnima, without realising that there is a scientific basis for it. But if an American or Englishman or Frenchman says that *Amavasya* has scientific significance, we take it as gospel truth. Such is our warped sense of values of modern age, polluted by all the things that the West is discarding.

Take the case of the thread (*poonool* in Tamil) which is associated with "the Brahman". Nowhere in any religious text is it written that only a Brahman can wear it, but all the social conflict has it as a symbol. Leave the controversy aside, when you wear the wet thread on the left side, its wetness is cooling the body. When a *dhoti*-clad man says it is good for the heart you will not believe it. But when about ten years ago, some Dr. John Smith (a fictional name) proved it in a scientific experiment on the East Coast of America, everyone in our country believed it as gospel truth.

This American doctor proved that the wetness acts as a coolant while the engine of the heart is pumping blood sometimes at excessive levels, indicating strain. But we won't believe our own people. This is a recent phenomenon. Historically speaking, since the Western values invaded our traditional ones, festivals have been reduced to nominal observance, where the sanctity (in scientific parlance importance) is lost and the inconsequential becomes the overriding consideration.

We talked about thread — the Bengali talks of *puja* holidays, we talk of *Ayudha puja*, *Vijayadashami*, and the northerners talk of *Dussehra*. Please tell me are they not the same, with one message of triumph of good over evil. What is *Ugadi* in Andhra and Karnataka is *Gudi padva* in Maharashtra. Lunar and solar calendars are used to good effect by blending them, using both, just as we have lakhs of temples and the twin faiths of Vaishnavism and Shaivism co-existing under the Banyan tree of Hinduism.

Take any festival in India especially those celebrated all over the country and you will find, the same, except perhaps for the name. Leaving local and regional festivals, most of which have something to do with geography, seasons, etc., it is all the same. Kashmir festivals are also celebrated elsewhere in the country, and the ever-present thread is still there. But more of that later.

22

Celebrating What, When and Why?

If you have a festival, can a fair be far behind? Or better still can the two ever be separated? No. A festival is observed or celebrated and a fair is the collective presence of people to give them a sense of participation. Visiting a fair with the family is a fulfilling exercise especially for the children. Take *Shivaratri* in Kashmir. The King, says *Rajatarangini*: "Flooded the people with presents just as Indra floods the earth with rain at the conjunction of planets". Feasts were held and dancing and singing performances given by the court artistes. Poetic symposia at which outstanding compositions of poets were applauded and their authors suitably rewarded, were regular features.

Another important festival still known but not so widely now was the Indradvadashi, held on the twelfth day of the bright half of Bhadra (September) which was the day of pilgrimage to the sacred sites ol Varahakshetra at Baramula (the seat of bloodshed, anarchy and killings now). This was naturally a festival of universal rejoicing coinciding as it did with the harvesting of the rice crop.

Doesn't that remind us of another harvest festival *Pongal*, thus, named in Tamil Nadu or *Makara Sankranti* in other parts of India. Social customs have over a period of time got interwoven into what was seen as religious practice and over the centuries has become a way of Hindu life. But modern thinkers and writers confuse this very often with religion. This festival of ancient Kashmir still observed by the elderly and the orthodox was also combined with the *Nagayatra* festival held on the fourth day of the same fortnight. A detailed account of the celebration is given by Shrivara in his biography of Sultan Zain-ul-abidin, one of the most famous Muslim kings of Kashmir after

Islam came to the valley in the fourteenth century.

Geography and climate can influence the way of living of the peopie. For instance, even the poorest of the poor need and have a shelter in the valley. Because the elements are harsh on the humans, the latter have to rnake provision for survival. An ancient tradition that matured into a festival deriving its origin from the practice of people leaving the valley in winter and coming back on the advent of summer is Asvayuja held on the fifteenth day of Ashvin (October). All this is described in detail in *Nilamat Purana*. People amused themselves by throwing mud at each other, by practical jokes.

The nearest modern equivalent of this festival is *Holi*, the festival of colours and this has been mentioned often by Kalhana the historian of Kashmir. People enjoyed this day by witnessing the Juggler's performances, Horseplay and exhibition of feats of strength. Al-Beruni has mentioned about this in his writings stressing the importance of festivals in ancient Kashmir. However, there is something in a festival that is forgotten by the modern generation that cannot be wiped out. People in India especially of the older generation would remember that the British always had a summer capital for their provinces in India. For instance, for Madras Presidency, the Governor would move to Ootacamund for the summer, and the Governor of Bombay would go to Lonavala or Matheran. While this has been officially given up in Independent India, our politicians still manage to have official meetings in hill stations at that convenient summer time.

And so it was in Kashmir too. After the Dogra dynasty took over consequent to the Treaty of Amritsar in 1846, the Durbar (court) of the King would move from November to May to Jammu and for the rest of the year stay in Srinagar. In those days it was called the 'Durbar Move', when selected departments of the Government would move from Srinagar to Jammu and return in May the following year.

And so it is to this day. In modern times, the movement of the Government departments is said to help the economy of the region by the influx of people from the valley to Jammu. And in summer, the tourists do provide the influx for the valley.

Nav Rath is the festival held on the first day of the bright fortnight ol Chaitra (March/April), when unhusked rice is to be seen in the morning. This is a prelude scientifically, speaking for the onset of spring.

Sons-in-law are invited for a feast and given presents before their return home. *Baisakhi* or *Vaisakhi* or Tamil New Year's day is the official day for the new year as per the Vikrama era. This coincides with the lunar calendar which is observed in a large part of India, along with the solar calendar.

Deepavali or *Diwali*, *Durga Ashtami*, *Rama Navami*, *Ganesh Chaturthi*, *Janamashtami* (Birthday of Lord Krishna) are, other festivals common to the Kashmir and the rest of India. There are however, in every place local shrines, which have a sanctity that is universal but by virtue of geography is very local.

Festivals are popularly, meant for the children but were we all not children once. That is the answer to what and why and the where of festivals. They serve to unite they serve to preserve and they serve to inculcate in us, the feeling of unity and with unity adjust it to the diversity that is India.

23

Valley and the Empire

YOU take a square, mount it on a body, mark the four parts and study it. If it is a map you have to find out the topography the physical features that help you to identify the mountains, the valleys and rivers, the passes especially in a mountainous area. The State of Jammu and Kashmir as it is known in the twentieth century is a combination of four different types of people and four different sets of physical features. Today, part of the State is under the illegal occupation of Pakistan but legally the state is still one.

Was the Kashmir valiey an independent kingdom at any time in History? Yes, few and far between in those days the kingdoms rose and fell at the point of a sword. Was it a part of the empire, any empire. Yes, in historic times, it was. And at times, from Kalhana we know that at one time the Kashmir Empire extended as far as Kanauj in the south and Tibet in the north.

Let us try to explore this unknown area if only, to know what it was like. Beginning in the south-east, we have the valley of Kashtvata, the present-day Kishtwar on the upper river Chenab. It is mentioned by Kalhana as a separate hill state at the time of Kalasa. Its *rajas* who were Hindus till Aurangzeb's time, practically retained their independence up to the beginning of the nineteenth century. The hill district of Bhadrawah lower down on the Chenab river had also its *rajas* who were till recent times paying tribute to the *rajas* of Chamba (now in Himachal Pradesh).

Says historian P.N.K. Bamzai:

The *rajas* of Chamba, ancient Campa, figure often in the

> Kashmir chronicles. Their territories since early times comprised the valleys of the sources of the Ravi river between Kangra, the ancient Trigarta and Kasthvata. The ancient Rajput family which ruled this hill state often intermarried with the Lohara dynasty which reigned in Kashmir.

To the west of *chamba* (in present-day Himachal Pradesh), lay the old chiefship of Vallapura, which is modern Bilawar. Its rulers are repeatedly preferred to in Kalhana's narrative. They retained their independence as petty hill chieftains till the rise of the Gulab Singh (Dogra dynsaty of which the present descendant is Dr. Karan Singh) in the mid-nineteenth century. The territory between Vallapura in the south-east and Rajadri in the north-west was and is still inhabited by the Dogras (presently identified as inhabitants of Jammu), a name traditionally derived from Vigarta.

When one travels by road (there is no railway as yet) between the winter capital Jammu and the summer capital Srinagar, one has to traverse the Pir Panjal range, a part of the Himalayas. During the nineteenth century, it was a briddle path and after the British engineered the sale of Kashmir valley to Raja Gulab Singh, and the advent of the automobile, a road was laid, appropriately named the Banihall Cart Road, as name that is still prevalent). The highest point where the automobile reaches, is about 9,000 feet and an arch was built by British Engineers in 1892. It was not a tunnel in the accepted sense of the world but an arch that gave some protection from the snow which would be blocked by snow for more than four to five months in winter. However, in the sixties, a new tunnel was built at a lower level about 7,000 feet, which has shortened the distance. When crossing the main Banihall pass (there is a small town by that name there) into the Kashmir valley proper, one can feel the difference due to mountains, snow and trees.

At the foot of the Banihall Pass is the territory known in ancient times as Vitasta. Temporarily, these small hill states acknowledge the suzerainiy of Kashmir, but during the greatest part of the period they held their own asserting their independence. Some of the hill states included the territories known as Darvabhisara, compromising the whole tract of the lower and middle hills between the Jhelum and the Chenab rivers (both these rivers are tributaries of the Indus). The combined names of the Darvas and the Abhisaras are found already in the ethnographical lists of the *Mahabharata* and the *Brihatsamhita*. A military chief of this region figures under the ethnic name of Avhisaras in the accounts of Alexander's Indian campaigns.

The most important of the hill states in this region was Rajapuri, which is today called Rajauri, very close to the line of Actual Line of control in the Jammu province of the State. Owing to its geographical location in the direct route to the Punjab, Rajauri was necessarily brought into political relations with Kashmir. Heun-Tsiang mentions this hill state to be a part of the territories of the Kashmir King on his time. From the tenth century onwards, we find the *rajas* of Rajauri practically independent rulers, though there were subsequent expeditions by the kings of Kashmir. The ruling family belonged to the Khasha tribe.

On the north-west, Rajauri is adjoined by the territory of Lokhara, the chief valley of which is now known as Lohrin. Lohara became important for Kashmir from the end of the tenth century onwards when a branch of its ruling family obtained the Kashmir throne. Subsequently, this branch of the family succeeded to Lohara, which became united, with Kashmir under the same ruler. The chiefs of this family are mentioned to have belonged to the Khasa tribe. As the ancestral home of the rulers, Lohara obtained an important position during the rule of later kings of Kashmir. Lohara was included later in the principality of Poonch (near the present-day line of Actual line of control in Jammu province of the State.) Like Rajauri, Poonch on the direct route to Punjab also finds mention in the historical chronicles of the period. To the north-west of Poonch, is the valley of Vitasta, a name also given to the river Jhelum by the ancients of the valley. From ancient times, it was held by the Kashmir kings as an outlying frontier post as far south as Bolyasaka, present-day Bultasa. Further down the valley up to Muzzafarabad (today under illegal occupation of Pakistan and the capital of the so-called Azad Kashmir). The territory was held by the fierce Khakha and Bomba tribes, who were subjugated by Gulab Singh only in the nineteenth century. This tract was known in ancient times as Dvarvati from which in modern designation of Dvarabidi has been derived.

Further to the west beyond Muzaffarabad lay the ancient kingdom of the Drusa, now known as the district of Hazara, also under the illegal occupation of Pakistan today (since 1947) . Its ruler is mentioned by name Arsakas in the accounts of Alexandar's campaigns. Heun-Tsiang while coming to the valley from the district found it a tributary of Kashmir. Drusa has been often mentioned in the *Rajatarangini* and is the present-day Abbotabad in West Pakistan.

Karnaha in the Kishenganga valley was small chiefship tributary to Kashmir. Drava, the tract above the junction of the Kishenganga river with the Karnah stream, included the famous shrine of Sarada, so often mentioned in the chronicles. The upper Indus valley to which a route lay from Sarada was outside the sphere of Kashmir political influence. Immediately, above Sarada, lies the territory known as Dardistan, or Dardadesa of the *Rajatarangini*. Its rulers who bore Hindu names more than once attempted to invade the valley. Daratpuri, 'The town of Darada', is the modern Gurez.

Crossing over from the headwaters of the Kishenganga river to those of the Dras river, we reach Ladakh district and the land of the Bhattas of the *Rajatarangini*. Sivara as historian of the period, refers to Ladakh and Baltistan as 'Little and great Bhatta-land'. The eastern frontier of the valley is formed by a mountain rage which runs from the Zoji-la almost due south to Kishtwar Along this range on the east lies a long narrow valley known in Kashmiri as Nmariv-wadwan. Its high elevation and rigorous climate are responsible for it to be thinly populated which is entirely Kashmiri. Beyond it to the east stretches the belt of high mountains and glaciers and to its south, we reach once more the territory of Kishtwar.

So, this is the story of how Kashmir looked like and what is was called then, the empires and valley. But what about the glitter, the commerce, the grandeur. The cities that that make civilisations thrive? Yes, towns and cities.

24

Is Civilisation Only Urban?

PONDER over a civilisation? How do we identify or evaluate it? The word brings to mind names like Patliputra, Ayodhya, Hampi, Vijayanagara, Taxila, Martand, Athens, Rome, Carthage, Alexandria, etc. They were in many cases city states and the grandeur and the greatness of the civilisation could be seen in the skill of its inhabitants, whether in the field of architecture or medicine or engineering or art, literature, dance or even music. History has left for us innumerable examples of such civilisations. From them, we can evaluate their contribution.

Village and village life has been a part and parcel of Indian civilisation and ethos. But like it or not, from time immemorial, it is the urban centre that generates knowledge and changing lifestyle as also social behaviour which seeps down to the rural level. It is so even now.

What were the urban centres like in Kashmir? In terms of geography, though the location of cities, towns has changed but little, yet their importance as centres of trade or the seats of Government varied from time to time for various reasons.

According to Greek and Roman historian, Kaspatyros was a city of Gandharians (those who migrated from Gandhara). It is believed that this was the name given to the capital of Kashmir kingdom. Kalhana says that Ashoka built the city of Srinagar which up to the sixth century AD was the capitai of the valley. King Pravarasena II built his city Pravarasenagar at the site occupied by the present Srinagar and moved the royal headquarters to it. Heun-Tsiang definitely mentions it as the new city in contrast to the old capital

Puranadhistahna or modern Pandrenthan. The history of Srinagar is as interesting as that of the valley. It was destroyed by fire several times and rebuilt. The houses were mainly constructed of timber then as also now. Kalhana mentions the splendour of its markets, gardens and lofty houses. There were no permanent bridges during the Hindu rule, but the river was spanned by a number of boat bridges like the present-day bridges that the army builds during war to span rivers, today called Bailey Bridges, named after an engineer of the Madras Sappers of the Indian Army who invented it in the late nineteenth century.

The *rajdhani* or the Palace of the Hindu rulers was usually located just below the second bridge. This needs to be explained geographically. The city of Srinagar today, as centuries ago, sits astride the river Jhelum, aiso called Vitasta. The river flows bisecting the city. On the banks are houses and native house boats locally known as Dhoongas.

Gradually to connect the two sides of the city across the river, bridges were built in the twentieth century. Though they are also referred to by their numbers, each one has got a name.

The modern city of Srinagar had seven bridges across the flowing Jhelum river. In modern literature, it is sometimes referred to as the city of the seven bridges. Earlier it was mentioned that the Hindu rulers had their palace just below the second bridge (meaning towards the third bridge). Each one of these bridges has a name. However, after 1947, two more bridges were added to it.

For instance, the bridge in question that is the second bridge is also known by another name Habba Kadal — it is named after a famous Kashmiri Muslim poetess. Habba Khatoon and Kadal is the Kashmiri name for a bridge. In the same vein, the first bridge is called Ameera Kadal, the first word Ameera meaning rich. It is a fact of history that fairly affluent people did and do live in that area. The fourth bridge in sequence is known as Zaina Kadal, named after Sultan Zain-ul-abuddin, a Muslim King of Kashmir known for his tolerance and piety.

With its landmark of Hari Parbat, a fort with a temple inside it on the banks of the Dal Lake and the Shankaracharya Hill with its imposing temple on top that got its name from the historic visit of Adi Shankara from the south, Srinagar, the city rests as it were at the feet of this temple. His visit was recorded for posterity by naming the hill as the Shankaracharya Hill, a name that continues till date.

The city was dotted with richly endowed stone temples, traces of which can still be found in sculptured blocks, pillars and images on the walls and embankments. Kalhana mentions the *ghats* and the bathing houses of the city Bilhana. Another historian found the city equally charming and surpassing in beauty other cities.

> For its coolness in summer and for the beauty of its groves, even those who have reached the garden of the celestials could not forget it.

Three important Kushana rulers namely Kanishka, Jushka and Huvishka built three imposing cities that still bear their names. Kanishkapura, Huvishapura and Jushapura are identified with the villages of Kaneshpura situated between the Vitasta (Jhelum river) and the Baramula-Srinagar highway, Ushkar, two miles to the south-east of the present town of Baramula off Zukur, five miles north-east of Srinagar. Of these three cities Huvishapura has often been mentioned in the chronicle and retained its importance for a long time as the headquarters of the Buddhist monks and also as the first town of note in the valley on its entrance from the Jhelum valley route. Huen-Tsiang, stopped here after passing the ancient gate of Baramula. It is mentioned by Al-Beruni, the Persian chronicler who accompanied Mohammed Ghaznavi on his variuous invasions of India, gives its exact location. Ruins of an ancient *vihara* and a *stupa* have been found near the village, as also a number of terracotta figures. *Rajatarangini* also mentions a town founded by Abhimanyu the son of the legendary Arjuna of the *Mahabharata* fame, which was located at Bemyun. King Nara's town Kinnarapura mentioned by Kalhana in connection with the legend of Susravas Naga, and situated near the modern town of Bijbihara was once a flourishing city with its markets full of fruits and vegetables and its *ghats* buzzing with loading and unloading operations of merchandise. It had lofty houses, parks and cool springs and surpassed even Kubera's town by the riches amassed there. But the wicked deeds of its founder King Nara brought on it the wrath of the Nagas and it was destroyed by them by lightning and fire. All this is history, but what is Bjibihara like today. Just a roadside town on the Jammu-Srinagar National highway. It recently figured in the national press for the killings that took place. It has become like any other village or small town dependant on the business provided by the passing passengers.

Near Nara's city, the town of Vijayeshvara built round the famous shrine of Shiva Vijayesha by King Vijaya. The city figures as the refuge of King Ananta and also the headquarters of the powerful Damaras of the southern district of the valley. The temple, which was surrounded by a high wall, was set on fire by Ananta's son Kalasa and later Bhikshacara.

It was here that several decisive battles were fought during the civil war between the later Lohara kings and several pretenders to the throne. About the middle of seventh century AD, Pratapaditya II, founded the town Pratapapura which has been identified as the present Tapar. Excavations conducted there recently have unearthed the foundation of an old stone temple.

Lalitaditya's capital city of Parihaspura, which he took pains to build on a lavish scale is now nothing but a desolate plain with scattered ruins lying about. It was systematically, destroyed and robbed of building material and objects of art. The city itself lost its importance also due to flood protection measures taken by Suyya, the engineer of Avantivarman, who changed the course of the Jhelum river, that had been flowing by it till then. Lalitaditya's grandson Jayapida, built the city of Jayapura which is the present village of Andarkot situated on an island rising from the Sumbal lake. The fortified city was the scene of the drama which saw the end of Hindu rule in Kashmir in the fourteenth century. Except for a few hamlets, there is no trace today left of it.

When we think of Kashmir, a number of things come to our mind, the beauty, the mountains, the lakes, etc., but there is one thing which we may have in our kitchen, thousands of miles from Kashmir that can remind us of the valley. SAFFRON. Yes, Saffron that since thousands of years would go along with other Indian spices to as far away places, as Samarkand, Persia, Egypt and even Rome.

And talking of saffron brings us to a small place called in ancient times Padamput, but today known as Pampore world famous for saffron cultivation, founded in the first quarter of the ninth century AD by Padma the maternal uncle of Cippatajayapida. Due to its central location in the valley, the town grew in importance and finds a frequent mention in the *Rajatarangini*.

The city of Avantivarman known as Avantipur, stood on a high spur of the Wastarwan hills on the right bank of the Jhelum river. Due to its strategic location, it has remained important and is often mentioned in the Samayamatrika of Kshemendra in the chronicles of Kalhana Raja and Shrivara. The large number of ruins remaining to the east of the present town Avantipur shows that in earlier times it used to cover a large area. The ruins are remains of the two old temples of Shiva Avanteshvara, Vishnu Avantisvamin, Surapura, the present Hurapura, the first stage from the valley on the old Moghul road, built centuries later by the Moghul rulers over the Pir Panjal Pass was founded by Sura, Avantivarman's able minister. It was the centre of trade.

Another important town founded during Avantivarman's reign was that of Suyyapur by Suyya. This is the present town of Sopore, which is often mentioned in the media as a centre of militant activities. Sopore is located on the river Jhelum immediately at the point that she leaves the Wular Lake, incidentally, the largest fresh Water Lake in Asia.

Avantivarman's son, Samkaravarman, founded the city of Samkarapura, is identified with the present-day town of Pattan, seventeen miles off Srinagar on the Baramula Road. The temples of Samkaragauris and Sugandesha by King Lalitaditya can be identified by their ruins at Pattan.

Kashmir also had queens in ancient times. One of them is Queen Didda who founded two towns Abhimanyakapur and Kankanpur. The former is not traceable. The latter is the present-day village of Kangan, 17 miles from Srinagar, on the road to Sonamarg.

25

An Ancient Tourist's Impressions

WHETHER it budget tourism or a rich man holidaying, visiting other places and countries is today taken for granted, what with inter-continental jets spanning thousands of miles in hours what used to take years just few hundred years ago. While today, we have hotel reservations, cars and the speed, the speed was very slow by today's standards, and it gave the travellers time to savour the delights of nature, come to know the natives more intimately, converse with them and through this interaction, learn about other civilisations.

India and China, being ancient civilisations, did have the intellectual interaction through scholars who travelled to each other's countries. While Ashoka sent many Buddhist monks to China, records of that are still available in China, Chinese scholar's works are also available for study.

Among the Chinese scholars who visited India, Fa-Hien was the earliest to come. His visit is recorded in AD 399. He was followed by a not so well-known scholar Fa-yong in AD 420. After him, came the well-known scholar Heun-Tsiang in AD 631. He was followed by You-Kong in AD 759. This Chinese scholar was so well respected in the valley of Kashmir, that they gave him the title of Dharma-dhatu.

While these are the prominent ones, a most interesting account of the Kashmir valley has been left behind for posterity by Yuan Chuang who was born in AD 602 a short distance from the town of Koku-shih. 'The boy grew up intelligent to the point of precocity', says his biographer Hu-uioll and had a serious but benevolent of expression and a sedate temperament, though rather lately passing years he stepped beyond the narrow limits of Chinese Buddhism.

Between him and the land of his dreams namely Kashmir, lay the deserts of Turkestan, a challenge he could not ignore. This was the year AD 629 when Emperor, Tal-Tsung sat on the throne, that Yuan Chuang set out on the road, already tread by Da-hein and Sing Yun and others. While others had curiosity as the motivating factor, Yuan Chuang was a scholar well equipped for the next sixteen years of voluntary exite: Whether it was discoursing with the unbelievers, or collating precious and rare manuscripts, he was a perfect example of cheerful stoicism. When he returned to China, he carried with him no less than 657 volumes of sacred books, seventy-four of which he translated into Chinese. He also brought relics of the Tathagata reverentially collected from all parts of India to honour the temple, where he continued his translation work. In 652, he had a *pagoda* constructed. Two years later, a deputation from Mahabodhi temple visited him. By AD 661, he had completed his work, which included the great *Maha-Prajna-Paramita-sutra* comprising 600 chapters in 102 volumes and in AD 664, he died.

What was his impression of Kashmir? Before we talk of that, let us take a quick look at the historic perspective.

At the end of the sixth century AD, the Gonanda dynasty was past its hey-day and its extinction was imminent. Baladitya, the last king of the Gonanda race married his daughter Anagalekha to an insignificant official named Durlabhavardhana. Possessed of unusual ability, Durlabhavardhana rose in influence and after Baladitya's death, he ascended the throne with the support of the powerful minister, Khankha. It was during his reign that Yuan Chuang arrived in Kashmir. Chinese records do speak of Tu-lo-pa that corruption of Durlabha to whom they attribute enormous prestige and authority over the border regions. The founding of the Karkots dynasty by Durlabhavardhana ushered in a period of prosperity for Kashmir, culminating in the glorious achievements of Lalitaditya Muktapida, a century later. Even in Yan Chuang's time, Kashmir was a politically very powerful land. This traveller records that Takshasila (Taxila) to the east of Indus, Drasa, Simhapur or the Salt range and the smaller hill states of Rajapuri (modern Rajauri) and Parnotsa had no independent rulers but were paying tribute to the Kashmir rulers. Corresponding with political stability and economic prosperity, the foundation of an exceptionally rich cultural life was also being laid at this time. Religious tolerance was a well-established policy of the Kashmiri kings and Buddhism flourished side by side. This was of course long before the onset of Islam, which came to Kashmir in the fourteenth century (1338).

At this point of time Kashmir had not only survived the ravages of Mihirakula, the Hun tyrant, but also was already moving towards a synthesis of cultural elements drawn from many sources.

Such was Kashmir in the year AD 631, a virile nation busy gathering up its traditions and preparing to build a great future, says the author of the authoritative book, *The Elephant and the Lotus*.

Travelling south-east from the Urasa, crossing mountains and rivers, he arrived in the valley entering by the stone gate on the western side. The King had sent his mother and younger brother with chariots and horses to escort the party to the capital. But Yuan Chuang was in no hurry. He visited many *sangramas* and stayed the night at the temple of Ushkar near Baramula where in the early twentieth-century Buddhist remains have been unearthed.

When he was only a mile from the capital Srinagar, he rested in a *dharmashala*. The king then met him in person along with his ministers and priests he was persuaded by the king to mount an elephant, and escorted him with standards and parasols, while incense and flowers filled the roads. The day after his arrival, the king requested him to inaugurate a reiigious conference. Mark that this was nearly 25 centuries ago. There were no fax machines, no typewriters and no Pitman's Shorthand, no telephones and no e-mail. The hosts, observing that he had no original texts with him, kept at his disposal twenty trained men to read the texts and copy them out for him.

Philosophical discussions with pragmatic questions bearing on the reality of life were held in those times with accommodation for the differing and the opposite view, while putting across the idea, the hypothesis or the belief for discussion, where logic, tradition, equity were tools to argue with. Yuan Chuang was praised by the chief priest with the words. "This priest from China possesses vast and immeasurable wisdom. He ranks with Vasubadhu and Asanga"

There is a historic irony about Kashmir and its tolerance of the world outside and those inside who were influenced by it. There was an atmosphere of religious catholicity and intellectual refinement and broadmindedness in Kashmir at this time. Consider it when just a thousand years later, it was marred by fundamentalist Islam that came with the sword and wreaked destruction and death on those who refused to bend to persecution in the name of religion.

During Yuan Chuang's visit, it must be remembered that the King was a Hindu, and Yuan himself was Buddhist, that he records was the religion of the minority in the Kashmir valley. But that did not prevent Buddhist scholarship from flourishing. What a contrast to the second half of the twentieth century. In the name of religion countries partitioned, forcible conversions, monetary attraction to change your faith.

Yuan Chuang came into contact with many Buddhist scholars, among whom were Vishuddhasimha and Inabandhu of the Mahayana School and Sugatamitra and Vasumitra of the Sarvastivadin School, while the Mahasamghikas were represented by Suryadeva and Jinatrata.

26

Enter the Dragon

As he sat cross-legged in a small wood on top of a mountain, he saw the stupendous grandeur of the valley, but no human beings. Madhyantika, one of the disciples of Ananda, Lord Buddha's blessed one had been meditating, demonstrating his spiritual powers. As he looked up at the lake facing him, he saw an extraordinary sight. A huge dragon rose slowly from the water and swam toward him. Addressing Madhynatika, the dragon, with his paws folded in submission said: "Maharaj, I have seen your powers and have total faith in you. Command me and I shall obey." Madhyantika was amazed but not surprised, for it was a part of the prophecy that Lord Buddha himself made.

After considering the dragon's offer, the *arhat* (*sadhu* or holy man) said "Give me a little space in the middle of the lake, just enough for my knees to stretch."

Promptly, the dragon withdrew the sheet of water and gave the *arhat* the land that he wanted. In the twinkling of an eye, the *arhat* increased the size of his body like Vamana in his Vishvarupam, and the dragon was unable to keep back the waters of the lake in spite of all his efforts. Ultimately, the Herculean effort of the dragon proved in vain and the lake became dry and a fertile valley.

Readers will recall the earlier explanation given about the origin of Kashmir valley and the legend of Kashyapa Rishi, as also the scientific explanation of the draining of the valley from a height of 7,000 feet after which the valley settled down in its dry form at 5,000 feet above mean sea level, which is its present attitude. However, this is the Buddhist lore, which as one can easily calculate would be about a thousand years after Buddha, when Buddhist missionaries had started fanning out in the eastern world to spread the word of the Buddha.

Now back to the dragon and the *arhat*. The dragon who was really a Naga, took to flight but before leaving asked Madhynatika for a place to live on. The *arhat* said "There is a pool to the north-west of this region. In this pool you and your tribe may live and prosper" Having, thus, obtained this vast land by his spiritual perfection, Madhyantika proceeded to establish five hundred Sanghranas. He invited people from the neighbouring countries to come and settle down in the valley. Sangharanas were a combination of seminary and a settlement around it. This is how Kashmir developed.

Earlier, it was mentioned that Lord Buddha had made a prediction about Kashmir. He also knew about Emperor Ashoka's connection with Kashmir. Yuan Chuang narrates that the mighty monarch, though deeply revered and having a loving regard for all creatures, after the Kalinga war, was unable to distinguish the true doctrine from the false. Along with the true *arhats* he also patronised some priests who were not sincere and were given to scheming. Among them was Mahadev, a learned and brilliant scholar, who wrote treatises, which were opposed, to the Law of the Buddha. Unfortunately, so goes the Chuang narrative, the Emperor came under the influence of this scholar and an assembly of five hundred priests was called at his instance on the banks of the far-away Ganga. But Mahadev's real purpose was to drown all these genuine *arhats*, but they having sensed the danger and flying through the air, came to the country of Kashmir and concealed themselves among the mountains and valleys and continued their meditations and studies. The Emperor, corning to know of this treachery, begged the *arhats* to return to the plains of India, but they refused and the Emperor himself came to the valley and built many monasteries and gave the entire country which was a part of his empire to the holy men (and today fundamentalists are questioning the connection or the link that Kashmir had and has with the rest of the country).

Yuan Chuang's account of King Kanishka (after whom an Air

India Jumbo jet was named) in the second century BC is by far the most accurate and valuable to the historian. Deeply affected by the prevailing dissension among the followers of the Buddha with regard to the interpretations of holy texts, Kanishka summoned a great council of scholars, priests and devotees. They completed their work by composing the *Upadesha Shastra* to explain the *Sutta Pitaka*. The next day, they composed the *Vinaya Vibhasha Shastra*, to explain the *Sutta Pitaka* and finally the *Abhidharma Vibhasa Shastra* to explain the *Abhidhamma Pitaka*. There was nothing in antiquity, says Yuan Chuang, comparable to this stupendous scholarly work undertaken in the valley of Kashmir at the behest of Kanishka. From the deepest to the smallest question, the assembly examined every point. In his own inimitable style. Yuan chuang says:

> The branches and leaves of the texts were investigated shallow and deep places were fathomed. After the deliberations were completed, Kanishka ordered the final discourses to be engraved on sheets of red copper, enclosed them in a stone receptacle and raised a stupa over then.

After Kanishka's death, Kritiyas captured power. They were considered to be foreigners of uncertain origin, and during their rule, the Land of the Buddha was ignored and the priests banished. Times were bad for Kashmir. Fortunately, help was at hand. King of Hisatala entered Kashmir with his warriors disguised as merchants and in the ensuing battle the Kritiyas were overthrown, and the good law established and the priests welcomed back.

Yuan Chuang mentions the four *stupas* built by Ashoka. In a *vihara* he met thirty priests of the Mahayana School. It was here that Sanghabhadra composed the *Nyayanusara Shastra*.

Yuan has also recorded a remarkable legend of the valley about an *arhat* who lived between the crags of a mountain in northern Kashmir. This *arhat* was exceedingly tall and fat, a veritable giant. His appetite was enormous. He ate and drank like an elephant and people railed at this everyday. When he was about to attain *nirvana*, the *arhat* called his neighbours to his bedside and explained the apparent contradiction between his gluttony and his piety.

He said: "In one of my former existences, I was born as an elephant. I lived in the stables of a King in eastern India. One day a shaman came to the city in the course of his wanderings in search of the sacred books of Buddha the *sutras* and the *shastras*. The king gifted me to this shaman and I was privileged to carry on my back all the holy texts that he collected. The merit I thus earned resulted in my being born as a human being. In a succession of human births I increased my merit until I became what you see me — merit with supernatural powers. But alas at meal times. I revert to my old habits and eat like an elephant."

Quite a tall story, thought all those gathered around his bed. But lo and behold, they saw him ascend into mid air and enter *samadhi*. His body emitted fire and smoke and when he attained *nirvana*, his bones dropped down and a *stupa* was erected upon them.

The above does not read like the reaction of a modern day tourist — but it is a record of the times — belief, legend, superstition, knowledge written by one who travelled by foot thousands of miles and wrote for posterity all that was current and prevalent then. If that is not history, then what is?

27

Trust in God, She will Provide

As the aquarian age dawned and modern education began to make its impact, a feeble demand began for the education of women. The suffragate movement in England in the nineteenth century was the result. Though its pace was agonisingiy slow (in Switzerland, women did not have the vote till the fifties of 20th century), women began to storm the male citadels more aggressively.

The recent case of women joining the Indian Air Force as pilots is an example. While we did and do have women doctors, lawyers, now politicians, and even engineers, the present-day scene in India is seemingly contradictory. Women have been treated as second class citizens not only in society, but also within the society in their homes. This is what provoked Gloria Steinhem to launch her war against the male chauvinism. While bra burning might have been a symbol of the strуggte, her crusade has a far deeper meaning. Why should a reporter be a newsman and not a newswoman? Why should God be given the male sex? Has anyone seen him to confirm that he is a man?

That brings us to the India of today. We have had a woman Prime Minister, Governors, Chief Ministers, High Court Judges and yet, the columns of the daily newspapers are filled up with news of gruesome happenings like rape, dowry deaths, kidnapping of women and a total lack of feeling or consideration for women.

And yet this is the land of Bharata, where woman is worshipped as Shakti, a deity, a concept that raises this sex to the heights of glory. Has anyone tried to bring such thinking back into the minds of the masses of this century and the coming century. Sadly no.

But what was the situation during the pre-Christian ancient erain the country. Let us look at Kashmir the paradise, lost now, but not for ever lost now, but reliving its past, if only to show what it was.

A striking feature of the political history of Kashmir during the Hindu period was the important and sometimes decisive role played by women in the affairs of the State and in society as a whole. There were queens or artistes or ordinary housewives or even inmates of a harem or courtesans who came into limelight. There is an interesting parallel to ancient Kashmir. Almost at the same time, in the Gupta period in the Indo-Gangetic plains women courtesans played an important role in the politics of the country.

The pyramidical structure of society that we have all over the world was there even in ancient times, as was the rich-poor gap. Women of upper classes received education not only of a general nature, but in diplomacy and Statecraft too. In Independent India, we now have woman Diplomats in the Foreign Service.

Bilhana, the poet laureate at the court of Chalukya king Parmadi (eleventh century AD) says in his monumental work *Life of Vikramankadeva*, while describing his homeland, that women of Kashmir spoke Sanskrit and Prakrit fluently. Damodaragupta's *Kuttanimata Kavya* talks of women being given sex education (contrast this with the attempt now to introduce sex education in schools after the West has done it), the art of dancing as propounded by Gharate, art as in the treatise of Visakhila, music as for instance in the works of Dantila. But this was not all. They had subjects like botany, painting, needlework, woodwork, clay modelling, cookery, instrumental music, singing and dancing. No wonder, in those times, women of Kashmir were as active as men in the discharge of their public duties. There is no evidence to suggest that women were kept in seclusion or relegated or sidelined to the background. The use of the veil was non-existent. Actually in India, this came into vogue with the coming in of the Muslim rule, primarily for protecting the womenfolk.

We find women sitting alone with the male nobles in the court of Harsha. We find them fighting alongside with men on foot and on hiorseback. People of this century have heard of the Rani of Jhansi or Rani Chenamma. Vijayamala, while retreating after the unsuccessful coup against her brother, king Harsha, was ably assisted by his brave wife, clinging to him on his horse, kept the pursuers at bay. Both of them and their horse swam across the flooded Vitasta (Jhelum) near Shadipur, and, thus, escaped to the country of the Dards. We have examples of heroism displayed by Queen Didda and later by Kota Rani.

For the past several centuries, at the time of coronation, the king if he is a male, is crowned and his wife becomes the consort. In the case of Queen Victoria and Queen Elizabeth II (the present reigning queen of England), their husbands were given the titles of Consorts. However, consorts are not given any responsibilities or powers.

But in ancient Kashmir at the time of coronation, Queens were anointed along with their husbands. For instance, Harsha, soon after his release from captivity was about to ascend the throne when there came before him Sugala, to claim her position as the chief queen. Several queens made their husbands' rule more successful by their wise handling of the administration and the royal treasury.

Queen Suryamati, wife of king Ananta, who finding that her husband was weak and about to be deposed by the rebellious Damaras, stepped in and by her wise and judicious selection of ministers and officials restored the confidence of the people in the king's administration. Later, she even forced the king to abdicate in favour of his son Kalasa, who she hoped would prove a more capable ruler, says P.N.K.Bamzai, the Kashmir historian.

Queen Didda dominated her weak husband Kshemgupta and virtually ruled in his name. Later, as regent and Queen, she controlled the destiny of the kingdom for half a century. *Rajatarangini* says:

> A Rani name Sarada was made use of for the purpose of giving her sanction to legalise the rebellion who had first conspired with the wife of the king designate.

This demonstrates the active participation of women in politics.

Kalhana, describes the chief Damara lords who remained neutral in the rebellion raised by Bhoja, another pretender to Jayasimha's throne. And therein mentions a Damara Lady who held the fief in her own right. That means she was given a *jagir* or area of villages to administrator and collect taxes on her own. No pre-puberty marriages were in vogue and intercaste marriages that are being touted today as something modern were already in vogue there almost a thousand years ago.

Widow marriages were permitted as we see from the case of King Pratapaditya II, marying the wife of a rich merchant. Kota Rani's marriage with Udyanadeva after the death of her husband Rinchin, shows that widow marriage was not taboo. *Sati* was not widespread. The Damara widow did not follow her husband's to the pyre.

Woman had their rightful place in society in ancient times, but in the interregnum, bad practices were introduced and the old system fell into disuse. Now, at an agonisingly slow pace, women have to fight for their rights, which were there even without asking in ancient India.

28

The Nuts and Bolts of Statecraft

GEOGRAPHIC boundaries have in ancient time varied due to the power of the king or his enemies. It was the empire, or the kingdom that mattered, not the people, or their language or ethnicity. Geography asserted itself during campaigns, as did the weather, but kingdoms would be as heterogeneous as Europe is today or Asia was a hundred years ago.

Ancient Kashmir, as a kingdom or an empire varied in size depending on who was ruling when. Generally speaking, the Hindu period under discussion had over generations stabilised itself laying down the guidelines for administration and the practice of Statecraft.

When King Damodara died, his queen Yashovati was made the regent of her infant son. The nobles and ministers grumbled at a woman being crowned queen, but Lord Krishna, on whose advice this was done, appeased them by reciting the following verse from the *Nilamat Purana*:

> Kashmir is Parvati, know that its King is a portion of Shiva. Though he be the wicked, a wise man who desires his own prosperity will not despise him.

This is the substance of the divine origin and powers of the kings about which Kalhana wrote at length in *Rajatarangini* that was prevalent until about a hundred years ago.

The king had to be humble and modest, though he had absolute powers. He had to be well-versed in sacred and secular lore. He received his training for the high office from his childhood and particularly when he occupied the position of *yuvaraj*. In modern parlance, it was time a probationary period or the king — designate just as the Prince of Wales in British Monarchy is in a way the king in waiting and under training. We get an idea of the strenuous training that a *yuvaraj* had to undergo from the autobiographical recollection of Shamkaravarman wherin he says:

> When I was a boy, I also had like you great affection for the people. My father (Avantivarman) was making me run along his horses barefoot with heavy armour, when hot and in thin clothing when cold, to make me feel the hardships that the common people had to endure, so that when I ascended the throne, I would not be too hard upon my subjects. But in spite of these practical lessons (he confessed), the concomitance of authority and despotism and I would entreat you not to behave in a harder manner than myself when you attain royal dignity.

Two things emerge out of this. One, the despotic nature of kings, which is quite well known. Two, though the post was hereditary, the kings were keen that their successors were worthy of them and training was the method by which they hoped that the successor would be worthy of them. In ancient Kashmir, though the office of kingship was hereditary, we have several instances of kings being placed on the throne either by the council of ministers or by a committee of nobles and Brahmans Meghavahana and Atrigupta were chosen by the ministers when Queen Sugandha (AD 904-6) wanted to nominate a fit successor to the throne and she sought the advice of the ministers. Similarly King Yasakara (AD 939-48) had to seek the approval of his ministers.

Contrast this with the present-day *maharajas*-those who rule over us and call themselves the servants of the people.

A council of ministers, very much like the present day one, except that the criterion was merit, was a must. In the pre-Ashokan period, the Government was of the same pattern as in other places in India with seven officials or ministers — the Judge, the Revenue Superintendent, the Treasurer, the Commander of the Army, the Envoy, the *purohita* and the Astrologer.

When Kashmir became a part of Ashoka's empire, the Mauryan system of administration was introduced. Jaluka, thus, increased the number of offices to 18 (like the present-day cabinet expansion) and, thus, according to Kalhana, inaugurated the constitutional system of Yudhishthira, meaning thereby the eighteen departments of state mentioned in the *Mahabharata* and the *Ramayana*.

This system continued till the time of Lalitaditya, who created five more new functionaries of high status, which were like court titles. Of all the ministers the Sarvadhikara or the chief minister was the most important and powerful and was directly chosen by the ruler himself. From Kalhana's account it would appear that the Prime Minister dictated the policy consequent to consultation of receipt of direction from the king, should he be a powerful one, or did it himseif if the king was weak.

Some of the most important portfolios were and are conforming to the present-day trends such as revenue, foreign affairs, religious matters, and education. The bureaucratic hierarchy was almost the same as today, without its defects, because appointments were by and large on merit and result-oriented.

All Hindu theory lays the greatest stress on the administration of justice as an essential part of the protection to which the people are entitled to from the Government. According to Manu (he seems to have fallen from favour in modern India), the king should normally preside over the law-courts and be assisted by experienced staff. The king was to hold court in a separate building and not his own palace.

There was of course, the chief justice and his importance was on par with that of the commander-in-chief. There were subordinate judges and judicial powers were exercised by other civil officers too. Justice was quicker, as paper work was less then that of today, and corruption was exposed soon, with the result a poor man could go to the Chief Justice directly and not only get iustice in time, but justice was seen by others to be on time.

Reflect for a while and think and marvel as to how ancient Indians did organise their state administration. It is ironic how the British system got so quickly ingrained in the Indian setting when the East India Company planted it on the Indian soil, but they (the Englishmen) did not know that bureaucracy was in the Indian blood and psyche. Looking at it today, it is strange that those practices given up in Britain, should continue to flourish long after it was given up there. The nuts and bolts of state craft. A police system has existed in all societies including Kashmir. The chief of the police was called Dandanayaka and espionage was one of the areas, which the police had to look after. Such was Kashmir. A look at the district and the village will complete the picture, but that is another story.

29

Timeless Wonders, our Villages

To those of the present generation the expression 'Panchayati Raj' is not new. The city dweller's contact with the Panchayat is non-existent, but he deals with its city counterpart, the municipality or the corporation. That in most cities in the country city corporations have been superseded point to a malady that is as old as India. Namely power and corruption.

The politicians want the administration to be run by the villagers themselves and the way they say it we know that they do not mean it. No politician would like to lose his power. So an escape clause has been incorporated in every bit of legislation ever since the slogan of Panchayati Raj became popular. Presiding over the village is the all-pervasive all-India services like the Indian Administrative Service (IAS) and the Indian Police Service (IPS).

But were our villages always like this, with the BDO gobbling up most of the money meant for the village or the politician grabbing his share first and then letting the smaller minions take their share. Corruption today in India has reached a proportion where it can be classified as a science. Take the hafta that is given to the limb of the law and order namely the police. Everything is graded according to the status of the person. But everyone gets a piece of the pie.

How has the Indian village survived the corrupt politician, the bureaucrat, the policeman or the minions of everything that becomes an assailant to the well-being of the village?

The answer to this lies in the resilience of the village — the village, the timeless wonder, who can take it all and yet survive on the barest of the minimum. Let us take a leaf out ancient Kashmir, because as we have stressed earlier, the unity of Hindu India was so strong in its thread that it has survived till this day.

If corruption was the bane of the society then, is it not so now? Yes, and that is what provoked the late Prime Minister Rajiv Gandhi to remark in sheer disgust and anger

> Out of every one hundred paisa spent in the villages, only ten paisa are genuinely spent on development.

Land was the main source of sustenance thousands of years ago, so is it today. Where you saw the bullocks toiling with the humans, you still see them today. Of course, there is the sprinkling of tractors and other gifts of science today.

You have the collector today in the south. The same officer is called the DM or the District Magistrate or the Deputy Commissioner in the north. Note the name collector, from ancient times, collection of revenue was the principal occupation of the Government as was the maintenance of law and order, for without the latter, there would not be the proper conditions for doing the same. What prevailed in ancient India was adopted by the British and adapted to the eighteenth and nineteenth century India, which we in Independent India have inherited and retained faithfully.

The Kashmir valley was divided into two administrative divisions namely Kramarajya and Madavarajya, also known as Kamraz and Maraz, which were put under the charge of a Mandalesa. A third division that of Lohara was added during the rule of the Lohara dyansty. These divisions were sub-divided into smaller units such as blocks in modern parlance and eventually the last unit was and is even today the village. Somehow neither in the ancient times, nor right down ages, on one has quantified what a village should constitute in terms of area or people. It is an elastic term, where fifty people in five square miles can make a village and 2,000 people in fifty square miles can also make a village.

Basically, administration was far less complicated than it is today. Two important officials of the village administration were the headman (*skandaka*), whose function besides collecting land revenue was to look after the welfare of the village and ensure a liaison between the individual villager and the Government — the modern BDO perhaps. He has since ancient times been an important link in village administration. In those days, the office was hereditary, generally, but subject to change by the superiors.

Remember the late Rajaji's education and employment scheme in the early fifties of the son learning the father's trade. In modern India, this was rejected, as would be if the headman collected the revenues and retained a part of it. Today, the revenue is transmitted to the Government, but the extra money is pocketed separately.

The other important official of the village was the village accountant known in those days as the Gramakayastha, who kept records showing the area of the holdings of the villagers, with their revenue assessment. He held his offfice at the will of Margapati, who 'paid bribes to him for the retention of his post', says *Rajatarangini*. Seems that not much has changed. Today, the bribing is still done but the ways of doing it may differ. The end result is the same.

From a critical study of *Rajatarangini*, it is clear that Kashmir had developed a well organised and efficient system of executive, revenue and judicial administration, which explains the continuity and maintenance of a smooth government even in times when there was a rapid change of rulers. With slight modification effected now and then to suit the fiscal policy of various kings, the administrative machinery for the villages and administrative units followed a uniform pattern throughout the Hindu period.

One aspect of administration needs to be clarified. Who manned the administration from the grass-root level to the highest theequivalent of the modern day chief secretary. It was the Kayasthas.

The word Kayastha need not be taken as an ingredient of the caste system. It is a kind of specialisation that spread the length and breadth of the country. They had other names, but it was skill-oriented rather than birth oriented. They became the backbone of the administration and for generations spanning rulers, Kayasthas became the synonym for civil service.

These timeless wonders, our villages, survived the Hindu period and the Muslim period and in 1947 when the country became independent, the basic tenets of administration from five thousand years survived and are even today retained. What is true of Kashmir is true of the rest of India as well.

30

Manning the Ramparts

ONE of the greatest weaknesses apparent, when one reads Indian history, is the lack of a doctrine for war. Dharam Uddh, or Holy war was never a concept, that could survive the ravages of time. Leaving the philosophical explanations aside, one can trace the reasons for the successive defeats of Indian kings by foreign invaders, Muslim firsts' and the British later, to the absence of tactics in the short run and strategy on a long-term plane. Perhaps one of the reasons was the unusual and unnecessary accent on muscle power without the complementary use of brainpower. A king was expected to be a warrior and lead his troops into battle. A chance arrow or a bullet would kill him and with that his army would face a rout. Built-up in the minds of his subjects as the be-all and end-all of everything, the loss of the king on the battlefield led to many defeats too numerous to enumerate here.

Belief in sheer numbers and the superlative aspect of size led to the false premise that war elephants and more soldiers make an army invincible. Tactics as an element of military operations came too late only at the time of Shivaji, who showed what fast cavalry, could achieve. Babar did the same thing at the first battle of Panipat and the victory gave his descendants the Moghul dynasty.

But a thousand years ago, there were people who thought and wrote about military tactics, strategy and organisation. In most kingdoms in India, it was the *senapati* or the commander-in-chief or *kampanadhipathi*, who rode out on offensive expeditions or defended the kingdom. But as Napoleon has said, a wise soldier takes stock of the geography round him, the weather prevalent, the rivers, the mountains, the passes and uses them to his advantage. Most kingdoms of India were in the plains. The Kashmir valley is surrounded by the great Himalayan mountain ranges, the highest in the world. Defending it against the foreign invaders was a vital task to preserve the kingdom from a sneak attack, for most of the attacks on this country especially from the north-west have been sneak attacks. Thus, the most important post in the military organisation of ancient Kashmir was that of the *dvarapati*, commander of the frontier passes. As the word *dvara* means door, it stands to reason that someone has to mind it and ensure that it remains under control. Watch stations and forts were established towards this objective and numerous passages in the historical chronicles show that they served the purpose of defence, customs and police administrations. They were garrisoned by troops under special commanders. That this post was irnportant is known, but the prestige that went with it, lends credence to the theory that should the *dvarapati* fail either in his capacity as a commander or change his loyalty, the fate of the kingdom would hang in balance and he would be the catalytic agent to change the fate of the state. Such a person required soldierly qualities and physical toughness, because the fight was not only against an enemy but also against the elements. What we today call below zero temperature was prevalent those days in that area with much more severity than today.

Kalhana mentions that the frequent transfers of the *dvar* office in the troubled times at the beginning of the twelfth century that the charge of the gate was never held by more than one person. It also signifies that unity of command over all the passes. The entire history of India, in pre-historic and historic times is dotted with efforts to defend itself never go for offence. Being enclosed in a valley and being coveted by rulers of Central Asia and Tibet, Kashmir had to perfect its military organisation for self-defence. During the Indo-Greek occupation, and also when it was a part of the Kushan empire, Kashmir received a thorough schooling in new methods of warfare. We learn from the chronicles about the preparations made by the astute king of Abhisara (present-day Poonch and Nowshera) in alliance with the famous Porous, the opponent of Alexander. With the extension of the Mauryan Empire to Kashmir under Ashoka, their military organisation and systems were adopted. Kalhana writes that the army of Kashmir comprised the traditional four arms — the elephants (today heavy vehicles), cavalry (today tanks), infantry and litters (in place of chariots in the plains) with their eighteen-fold divisions. It is not surprising that today the basic tenets of military organisation remain the same. A word about the elephant. Ever since man started training elephant as a beast of burden (to which use it is even today put in logging operations), the elephant was also trained for war. War elephants were used both for carriage, attack and defence. But quite often, they were more a liability than an asset in battle. All of us have read what happened to Ibrahim Lodi at the battle of Panipat, when he was riding his war elephant. King Harsha, who came out in person to fight the rebels in Srinagar had to suffer a terrible defeat when his war elephant hit in joints by arrows from the rebei forces, raised a trumpeting roar and turning back trampled down with his feet his own force. Attacked by the elephant, which had turned hostile, the foot and horde of the army were routed.

While the horse was the aeroplane of the army, with its speed and mobility, the infantry soldier was the main fighting element in defence or offence. This is even so today. They had swords and lances and today they have carbines and hand held Stinger missiles, but actual conquest or defence of a piece of land is still to be done physically and none can replace the infantry soldier. A curious aspect of the Kashmir infantry was that they were taught the ancient version of using missiles with a sling as the launch vehicle. With a round but sharp stones tied to its end, they flung the stone with unerring accuracy at the target. Perhaps a Stinger missile of the ancient times. Kalhana records that the strength of Jayapida's army comprised eighty thousand, whereas Lalitaditya had over a lakh. Vincent Smith, the British historian, writing about Chandragupta Maurya says that "incredible though they (figures of its strength) may seem at first sight, they are justified by our knowledge of the unwieldy, hosts used in war by Indian Kings in later ages" For instance, Nunez, the Portuguese historian, who was contemporary with Krishna Devaraya, the Maharaja of Vijayanagar, in the sixteenth century (1509-29 AD) affirms that the prince led against the Kingdom of Raichur (now in Karnataka) an army consisting of 703,000 soldiers, 32,600 horses and 551 elephants besides camp followers.

There was no caste barrier for recruitment into the armed forces, nor was there any theory of the martial classes that the British inflicted on us. Brahamans, Kshatriyas, Vaishyas and agriculturists were in the army and Chandalas and Domas also took to military service. Kashmir kings also frequently recruited soldiers from the various tribes in Punjab and Frontier provinces as also Chamba, Kangra, Lahaut, the last three being in the modern Kashmir Army before 1947. And today there are two regiments in the Indian Army namely the JAK Rifles and JKLI, where recruitment is not only from Jammu and Kashmir but also from Himachal Pradesh.

Ancient system of defence depended largely on forts built at strategic points to stand prolonged siege. Tanks were built for storing water and these forts were garrisoned by small detachments of trusted troops, roughly equivalent of the *killadar* system of troops, which was prevalent till the beginning of this century.

In the valley proper, there were forts of two types — one land forts and two water forts. The land forts were generally built on spurs of hills. As an instance of water fort we have the one built by Jayapida in his new town of Jayapura. It was like an inner castle, and occupied a strong position being situated on a plateau surrounded on all sides by water. It was here that Kota Rani, the last Hindu ruler of Kashmir was besieged by and surrendered to the forces of Shah Mir. Strangely enough, Srinagar has had no fortification, except perhaps the fort on the Hari Parbat hill which was built as recently as the nineteenth century.

> We can attribute this exceptional position of Srinagar to the great natural advantages of its site. The frequent sieges which Srinagar underwent during the last reigns related by Kalhana, gives us ample opportunity to appreciate the military advantages of the position of the city. With the exception of the comparatively narrow neck of high ground in the north, the city on the right riverbank is guarded on all sides by

> water. On the south, the river forms a formidable line of defence. The east is secured by the Dal Lake and the stream, which flows from it. On the west, there stretches the broad marshes of the Anchar Lake close to the bank of the Vitasta, says the historian Auriel Stein.

Such was Kashmir — it looks the same today, except for blood that is flowing not through the veins, as it should, but spilled in senseless killings.

31

The Curse of Taxes

In Independent India, only the urban taxpayer and that too the income earner does not see his entire salary. Its tax, that is on the same income generated is deducted at source. So, if he is earning Rs. 9,000 he does not see the entire mount. But the one section of Indian society, which is exempt from income tax, it is the agricultural sector, where predictably it is the rich farmer who benefits, since the landless labourer does not even have the benefit of provident fund. But in ancient times, the source of revenue for the state was not from any other major source except land and that too in kind. There were not many forms to be filled, and what went to the official's register was the record for posterity as to the amount levied and collected.

It was mainly land revenue that paid for the king's palace, his army and his public works expenditure. In ancient Kashmir, the average rate of tax in terms of land revenue was one-sixth, about 16.5 per cent. However, with increasing instability of administration during and after the tenth century AD, revenue receipts dwindled and successive kings used all kinds of unjust methods of collection.

An impoverished people with an unjust administration is seen as collective oppression by the state on the people. A revolt is the next logical step. However, while no organised revolt took place, individuals protested in their own unique manner. But all the kings were not unreasonable. It was during the peaceful reign of Jayasimha that some of them were abolished; but not before a popular burst of public anger.

The people of Avantipur observed a solemn fast against the policy of the powerful minister Siddartha, who was increasing the imposts (Gandhiji's fast came centuries later).

But this made no impression on the obstinate minister. Finally a youth named Vijayaraja, historian Kalhana's contemporary, taking recourse to terrorist methods, attacked Siddartha with a dagger and grievously injured him. Vijayaraja disdained to flee although he could have done so, and announced that he had stabbed the minister.

However, there were enlightened rulers as well. Lalitaditya and Avantivarman undertook extensive irrigation projects. Suyya's (his engineer) expenditure on clearing the bed of the Jhelum river at Baramula of rocks and silt, was one of them. It seems that large amounts were also spent on the maintenance also. It seems that large amounts were also spent on the maintenance of roads and bridges. Public bathhouses on the Jhelum in Srinagar were built as also schools and hospitals. Most of the educational institutions and hospitals, as also bridges and roads were built and maintained by the kings of Kashmir right up to 1947 and even today many of these institutions owe their origin to the foresight of the *maharajas* of Kashmir.

It may interest the reader to know that being a State dependent mainly on agriculture, Kashmir developed a unique institution not existing in any State or province of British India before 1947. The concept of the State holding buffer stocks of paddy came from the brilliant mind of Raja Narendra Nath Kaul, the Revenue Minister of Maharaja Pratap Singh, who purchased paddy from farmers in what today is called creating buffer stocks.

He created a department called 'Shalee store'. Shalee in Kashmiri meaning paddy and to this day it exists and performs the role that was meant for it almost eighty years ago. What the Food Corporation of India (FCI) does in buying buffer stocks from farmers and keeping it in reserve owes its origin to Raja Narendra Nath Kaul's pioneering effort in Kashmir.

Kalhana says that villages were wholly absorbed in agriculture and there was great pressure on land. Of course, the main crop was paddy, and though a thousand years or more have passed since then, Kashmiri's staple diet even today is rice.

Unlike in the plains, where you have two crops minimum per year, Kashmir valley due to a prolonged winter has had from time immemorial only one crop. Sowing operations begin in the month of March and by the month of September, the fields are covered with ripened paddy. So this was and so it is today. Oxen were used to plough the fields and harvesting was done in October after which the ceremony for sowing the new crop called *Navana* was performed. In Tamil Nadu, the harvest festival in January is *Pongal* and it corresponds to that though the climatic difference explains the difference in dates. There is evidence the cultivation of barley and pulses was there too.

Today, when you go to the market and see ripe apples for sale, the first thought that strikes you is Kashmir. Fruit cuitivation seems to have been practised from ancient times. We have mention of grape gardens in the *Rajatarangini* and though centuries have passed, we still have them, even if technology may have changed. Heun-Tsiang, who visited Kashmir in the seventh century AD, remarks that the country was a good agricultural one and produced abundant fruits and flowers. Among the fruits were pear, peaches, grapes and apples.

One area, where even today Kashmir has a monopoly is Saffron. Known as Kashmiriraja, by Kalhana, one of the five things for which Kashmir was famous, saffron was also used as an ingredient in Greek medicines and cuisines and it continues to be used in Kashmir. There is a legend about how saffron came to Kashmir and continues to be used. On the plateau of Padampura (modern Pampur) the first bulb was planted by the famous physician Wagbhatta who received it as a gift from Naga Takshaka on his being cured of an eye disease. The elaborate method of his cultivation in well-prepared beds seems to have been followed from ancient times.

To sustain agriculture, one needs infrastructure. One cannot think of modern agriculture without irrigation and a lot of attention was paid to it. Irrigation canals played a significant role in it. Vast irrigation projects were completed during the reign of almost all the kings such as Suvarna, Damodara, and Lalitaditya. But the most important contribution came from brilliant engineer minister Suyya during king

Avantivarman's reign. He is said to have embellished all regions with an abundance of irrigated fields which were distinguished for excellent produce.

Land is still with is, though the militant is today threatening those living on it. The farmer was there then, he is still there today. Some things, as they say, never change and land is one of them.

32

Whose Money is it Anyway?

THERE was a popular talk show on a foreign TV network, entitled 'whose line is it anyway?' It is unusual, in that, the actors without props show situations that brings out the humour in them. The idea behind the title, is that if there is freedom of expression, it is for all, and not the few favoured ones.

Similarly, money, it may be the root cause of all evil, as any holy man will tell you, but without it this big bad world will not be able to run. But corruption is a different ball game altogether. In modern context, its meaning and content has changed. The dictionary says that corruption means getting something done by offering bribes. And something is either a thing or a piece of paper, needed either as a sanction of legalising something which smells fishy, or very plainly getting something very genuine done soon enough without any hassles, for which the harassed honest person has to pay extra money if only to save time, and tears.

The British when they ruled us, did not lose any opportunity of telling us how corrupt we, the Indians were. But they conveniently with a straight face and a stiff upper lip (for which they are famous) forgot all about the plundering of Clives and Warren Hastings, not to mention the Kohinoor diamond which even today reportedly adorns the crown of Queen Elizabeth II.

You must have certainly heard of corruption. After ail, it begins practically on your doorstep, when you desperately want a gas cylinder and the guests are waiting for dinner. Show me any government office, where the peon will open the door to the boss chamber without money greasing his palm. The iate Mrs. Indira Gandhi once said that

that corruption is a worldwide phenomenon. So it is and in our country with our hoary past, of which we are very proud, corruption has been a way of life, and has accompanied us from as long ago as you would like to go back to.

When jobs were hereditary, the confirmation in service was a milestone not the training, because that came with parentage with the father breaking his head to make his offspring presentable for the job and not the other way around. Today the only difference is either a caste certificate or a recommendation letter or plain buying up the job.

How was it in ancient India? Were all the people honest, good and pious. Yes, one would venture to state that most of them were, since opportunities for making money were few, but the few who had the power, did make money.

In ancient Kashmir, so the story goes, there was an extremely clever, scheming and very intelligent officer. Wherever he was sent, he did a good job, but the CID report on him to the king was: yes, he is very efficient, but is thoroughly corrupt. In a rage, the king transferred him (the word is modern, and in those days, it was shifted him). But whichever department he was sent to, he managed to make money. And the reports kept flowing.

In desperation, the king sought the advice of the Dewan. "Maharaj, we should send him to such a department, where there can be no possibility of making money."

"Yes, but which one?", the king asked.

"I shall have to think this over, Sire."

" Yes you do that and report to me tomorrow morning."

The queen was disturbed to see the king in such a thoughtful mood and suggested a *shikara* (boat) ride on the Dal Lake. Rather diffidently, the king agreed and the two set out. It was dusk and the gentle breeze stroking the face was the ideal setting for a romantic evening, but it was not to be. The queen tried to cheer him up, but he stared ahead, totally glum.

33

Trade Links Across the World

TRADE in modern times is linked to industry. Industry as was know it today conjures visions of giant factories belching smoke and producing consumer items for the world markets.

But before the industrial revolution ushered in the modern age, there was industry and there was export and import, even when there was barter economy in vogue. But international trade as we know today, with cargo jumbos spanning the continents worldwide in hours that once took months and years was not there. Ancient Kashmir had, far flung political and cultural contacts with distant corners of India, central Asia and Tibet and China. Under Ashoka and later Kanishka, Kashmir became part of vast empires and being geographically placed at a strategic position, sitting astride as it were on the fulcrum of Asia, became a meeting ground of caravans from the plains ol India and the distant cities of Central Asia.

Besides being a modern day free port, Kashmir also exported its own products. Woollen goods, saffron, kuth used in medicine making and small quantities of silk. It has not been exactly recorded as to when mulberry cultivation started on a commercial scale and when the production of silk began, but from-various descriptions in the chronicles, we come to know that silk was one of the products of export.

Added to this, the demand for Kashmir saffron was very great in the Indian market. It is even so today. Heun-Tsiang noticed woollens being worn by the inhabitants of the northern regions of India. As the wool for the manufacture of shawls comes from the highlands of Tibet, the trade with that country has an ancient origin. In recent times, when the conflict with China broke out in 1962, this link got snapped, but even now the possibilities of trade are tremendous, with the warming up of the ties between India and China. One can today understand how Kashmir came to be identified with and famous for its handicrafts and woodwork and paper mache apart from its natural beauty. Whereas, raw *pashmina* (wool) was an item of import, the finished product namely shawl and other items of clothing were for export. Grapes were exported to northern part of India. We have an echo of this in the *Ain-i-Akbari*, the chronicles of Akbar's time in which Abul Fazal, the chronicler mentions that 'Kashmirians bring grapes on their backs in long baskets'."

International trade in those hoary days may have been very slow by today's standards, but it was a continuous process that kept the wheels of industry churning, howsoever, slow they may seem today. Among the articles of import in Kashmir were salt, spices and cotton and silk from the rest of India as also precious metals and copper and brass for coinage. Marco Polo mentions that coral, which was carried from the Western parts of the world, had a better sale in Kashmir.

Internal trade in the valley was confined to foodgrains, cattle, farm implements, earthenware and other metallic vessels and minor farm and industrial products. The principal centres of trade in the valley were Puranadisthana, Parihaspura, etc. Kerala in India is a fine example of using natural resources and physical features for commerce. A lot of commercial activity such as transportation of goods is carried on by boats on the internal waterways. In Germany from time immemoriai, the Rhine has been a source of sustenance to the people of the country. Being a big river, ships also ply on it and trade is carried on through this vital waterway. In a way, it is the lifeline of Germany. In the Indo-Gangetic belt, the Ganga, is a waterway for carriage of goods and passengers.

In Kashmir most of the internal trade of the valley was carried by the river Jhelum and its tributaries. In the chronicle of Kalhana, there is mention of river journeys, boats and bridges and *ghats* or landing places. When king Kalasa, who was staying at Vijakesvara, wished to pass his last days at the temple at Martand, he was 'carried by the water route in boats, along with his ministers etc.' and from there to the nearest *ghat* or landing place of Martand, which would in modern terminology for identification be Khanabal, that is today on the main route from Jammu to Srinagar.

When one talks today of the physical unity of India from Kashmir to Kanyakumari, one fails to realise that it was there centuries ago. And the proof of it is the chronicles of the period. During the reign of Pratapaditya II, 'The land was full of merchants of different wares coming from all regions.' during the reign of Ananta, a merchant from the plains of India was entrusted by king Bhoja of Malwa to build a wall round the spring at Kapeteshvara and also to send its holy water to him everyday in glass jars. He also supplied betel leaves to King Ananta and by trading in different commodities became so rich that when Ananta was in financial trouble, he became the king's creditor and took from him precious presents as a security for money, which was due to him.

One might today become curious to know as to what the currency was called. Remember paper currency came to India during the British rule, but before that it was the coin the humble brass or copper coin or the gold coin. In ancient Kashmir, it was Dinara the rough equivalent of the rupee. The currency was basically copper. From the coins, one gets an idea of the exact dates of the rulers in the absence of any other historical data.

Kashmiris have from time immemorial due to climatic reasons been non-vegetarians, but among the Hindus there were taboos for eating meat on certain days considered holy. It is peculiar that no beef or chicken was served in those times. Only mutton was the dish, and the fresh river fish.

It is a fact of life that in the mountainous regions not only in Kashmir, but also in Himachal Pradesh, the hills of western UP and the north-east, even the poorest of the poor had a roof on the head. And the construction of the houses was such, that in summer, it was cool and in winter, a native kind of insulation provided to ensure warmth.

Most of the Kashmiri families even to this day divided their house into three parts. The ground floor was the living room where all the members sat talked and ate together. The kitchen remained during winter on the ground floor. The bedrooms were on the first floor and on the second floor it was a replica of the ground floor. A common sitting or living room with kitchen for use during summer. The shifting was done in November and May and to this day it continues in the old type of houses.

While Kashmir went through periods of peace and prosperity which remained etched in history, let us look at the contribution in terms of philosophy, culture and religion.

34

Crime, Justice and Punishment

WE invoke the name of Gandhi on every occasion but immediately thereafter forget him. We know what he meant by patriotism but it has just remained a word. It was a generation who understood in practical terms the meaning of country before self.

Can the present generation recall how many served the country sacrificing their jobs, education and peace of mind of their families? In the last 50 years how much have we done so that we can say that we have kept the nation above self.

Patriotism is a word, which we mouth but don't do much about. Those of us who live in Bangalore may have had the occasion to visit the Vidhana Soudha (State Secretariat) and notice at the gate the saying that 'Government Work is God's Work'.

By using God's name the attempt is to make it universal but the essence is to make it apply to us in the context of an independent nation. In the last 50 years, what have we done to make a reality of such a slogan. We have the leaders and the led. The former is to set an example to the latter to follow.

Today if the minister makes a blunder and causes loss and suffering to people, what is the punishment? The greatest punishment is for him to resign his ministership. Is that enough? Even when an official like Police Inspector breaks the law, all that is done is to transfer him. Is that enough?

Let us look at Ancient India and see what punishment was given to those in authority who should have set an example.

According to Manu, a king should be fined a thousand times as much as a common person for the same offence. (*The law of Manu* VIII, 336) He also held that the upper castes had to follow higher standards of conduct than the lower and, consequently, their crimes were to be considered more heinous. For example, as the penalty for theft, he prescribed that a Shudra should pay a fine equal of the stolen goods, while the Vaishya, Kshatriya and Brahman should pay sixteen, thirty-two and sixty four times the value respectively.

Granted, the world has become more humane and such punishments are not awarded in today's India, but the question of responsibility needs to be addressed rather urgently as more than 70 per cent Indians today have been born after the British left and do not have an idea first hand of the freedom movement.

"Freedom cannot be inherited in the bloodstream, each generation will have to defend it and fight for it. Then alone will it survive to be passed on to the next generation." We have to ensure that when we talk of nation before self we look at the practical aspect and try as individuals to do unto others what we would have others do unto us.

King	1000 times
Brahman	64 times
Vaishya	32 times
Kshatriya	16 times

The present generation, influenced as it is by Western thought has given up most of the rules and ethos under which generations of Hindus were brought up from time immemorial. When Gandhiji, called by the British Tories led by Winston Churchill as the 'naked fakir', resorted to fasting as a means of protest, the rulers laughed at him. But led by fasting he took the next step which did not bring forth any laughter and that was mass action.

What Gandhiji did was what ancient Indians resorted to as a weapon, a device and a methodology to set right the wrongs perpetrated on the individual or society. In ancient Kashmir as in the rest of India, the king was the chief executive of the state. His decisions were obeyed, but to arrive at them in a fair and impartial manner he had to undergo the same rules and regulations that he mandated for others to obey.

Very often bureaucracy, then as now, came in the way of dispensing justice. As an umpire, the king had to ensure that bribery and corruption did not come in the way of dispensing justice. Today, we have the device of a writ petition, which has to be submitted through a lawyer in the High Court or other courts. The system in those days was much more simple and direct. Today access to the Prime Minister or President is restricted but in those days it was more direct. One did not have to stand in a line to ask for an appointment with the king. Business of the public was conducted in public in an open court.

Fasting as a mode of protest was very much in vogue and very often the king would come to know often injustice done to any one of his subjects for which he was fasting and for which he wanted justice.

Knowledge and education in ancient Kashmir, as in the rest of India was verbal through the word of mouth. Written records began with palm-leaf writings and those are the only written records that have survived the ravages of time. One of the most elaborate descriptions of Kashmir of the tenth and eleventh century AD comes to us from *Rajatarangini* written by Kalhana. It is the only written record that can be called history about Kashmir tracing the princely dynasties and politics of the period. *Rajatarangini* also describes the system of Government principles of criminal, justice system, customs, traditions and the verbal folklore.

The period that Kalhana describes is about four to five hundred years before the fourteenth century when Islam made its appearance in Kashmir.

The present-day detective fiction owes its origin to a little known book that appeared in the nineteenth century under the title of Moonstone. Modern crime detection in later fiction of Sherlock Holmes and Agatha Christie owes the details to the development of crime detection the nineteenth and twentieth centuries. However, crime has been with us ever since Adam offered (perhaps with ulterior motives) the apple to Eve. In ancient Kashmir detection of crime was the responsibility of State. There were departments, which correspond to those that we have today.

Bureaucracy has been disliked from the beginning of time by those who had to suffer under it. Today we do have the courts as they had then. Today we have the right of appeal to higher courts and final appeal to the Supreme Court of India.

In ancient Kashmir the king was the final court of appeal. A citizen did not have to stand in line for an audience with the king. The citizen had his weapon — a peaceful weapon that could turn lethal. Fasting unto death was a practice in vogue during the reign of King Yasaskara (AD 939-48). He was a wise king who practised what he preached. He enforced the laws impartially. "The land became so free from robbery that at night the doors were left open in the bazaar and the roads were secure for the travellers", says U.N. Biswas in his well researched monograph on crime and detective sciences in ancient Indian literature, published by the Asiatic Society, Calcutta (1987).

Voluntary starvation was used as a means of bringing to the king's attention the wrongdoings of his officials or any other form of cheating or wrongdoing by others where the victim did not get justice at the hands of the officials. One such instance illustrates this.

A merchant resorted to voluntary starvation. As the king had given instructions to his officials that instances of voluntary starvation should be brought to his notice the merchant was produced before the king. Narrating his story the merchant told the king that he was a rich person who became a pauper. He decided to sell of all his property and travel abroad. For the maintenance of his wife he kept a well fitted with stairs. He was confident that his wife would be able to live well by the rent given by the gardeners who in summer placed flowers and petal leaves in the cool well. After wandering for 20 years he returned home with a small fortune, but could not find his wife. At last he found her working as a maidservant. When he asked why she said, after his departure the merchant to whom he had sold his property drove her out. Finding no way to get back his property he was depressed and began Prayopavesa (voluntary starvation), but the judges before whom he put his case decided against him.

He went to the palace and told the guards that he would die at the door of the king and prayed that the king should decide his case. After hearing from the judges who had decided against the merchant, the king decided to try the case himself. The judges had held that the merchant was a forger and that he had sold the well and the stairs along with house. The king asked the defendant for his ring and on a pretext went into the other room. From there he sent an attendant to the merchant's house with the ring as identification and asked for the account book for the year in which the sale deed had been executed. The accountant at the defendant's house gave the attendant the account books and kept the ring.

The king thoroughly perused the account book and was surprised to find that and entry of 1,000 dinars, which had been paid to the official record keeper which, meant that the official had been bribed. The merchant had bribed him to write a 'Sa' in the place of 'Rae'. The words of the deed as quoted are supposed to have been: 'Sepankupasahitam vikritam grata': The document ought of have had *ratitam* instead of *satitam*, with the meaning: " The land is sold without the well". The king showed the account book to the assembly and explained the fraudulent recording of the terms of the deed.

The case was decided in favour of the plaintiff and the defendant was exiled.

A similar case was brought before the same king wherein the complainant had left his home and after many years returned after earning 100 gold coins. As the country was free from robbers he slept under a tree. Next morning he went to the well to wash himself and accidentally the garment containing the gold coins fell into the well. He was sad and wanted to die, but a stranger offered to go down the well and recover the gold coins. But he demanded a payment. In his utter helplessness the man told the helper 'whatever seems right to you, let that be given to me from it'.

The man got down into the well and came up with the coins. The helper paid the man only two coins and kept rest for himself. When the man protested those around him said that he had agreed to the terms and he had no grounds for complaints. The king called the helper and asked him about the case. The king decided the case by giving 90 coins to the man who had lost them and 10 to the helper. He explained his decision thus: instead of saying 'whatever you give let that be given', the version given by the helper, the owner of the coins had said, 'whatever seems right'. The owner had put the onus of fairness on the helper who got greedy. But words uttered by the owner of the coins convicted the defendant.

35

The Generation Gap
(Indian Style)

Mental and Social attitudes, it is recognised all over, have changed and modern life has taken a toll of our adults and children. In the past it was a continuous line that were born, grew up served and retired and passed on very often dying in the same house where they were born. Today technology, distances have created stress which manifests itself in different ways. Children become disobedient, the young don't understand the old and the old feel left out and insulted by the young. Present-day psychologists' call it the generation gap.

"Appa, What is that?"

'What is what my son?"

The child is sitting in his father's lap stretched his tiny arm and pointed at the mulberry tree in backyard adjacent to the house.

The father looked and identified the tiny mynah (sparrow family) sitting on a branch and cooing to its young one on its nest.

"That, my son, is a mynah. It is a bird."

"It is a birdie, it is birdie, it is a birdie."

"Yes, it is a birdie" said the father with a satisfied smile.

But, the little boy of five would not let go. He kept on asking the same question.

'What is that on the tree?"

And got the same answer from the patient father who resigned himself to being patient with his child.

Years passed. The child grew into a man and the father grew old. The young man got married and had a good job.

Twenty-five years passed. The father sat in the same corner and looked at same mulberry tree. His eyes were not sharp now. Suddenly, he saw something white on the same branch where years ago the mynah had sat. It was white in colour and moved suddenly.

Just at that moment, his son stepped into room.

"My son, can you tell me what that is on the branch of the tree."

With an impatient gesture, the son barely glanced at the tree and said, "it is just a cat".

"But I think, it is ....

"I told you it is a cat. How many times must I tell you that? You think I have no other work, but to answer your silly questions": With that he just left the room. The father sat quiet, ciosed his eyes and thought for a while. A few minutes later, his wife came into the room with a hot cup of tea. He accepted the cup with his *phirin* (gown) edge in his right hand and sipped the liquid.

"You are very quiet today", asked his wife.

He did not reply, but gestured with his left hand towards a small box, which contained papers. The wife brought the box and he opened it and found what he was looking for. Meanwhile, his son after sometime came into the room and spoke normally to his father.

"My son, can you help me with this. Just open this dairy on this date and read what is written on it."

Slightly puzzled the son obliged and this is what he read. "My son today asked me 29 times what the bird was on the tree and I obliged." When he read this, the son was thoroughly ashamed and begged his father's forgiveness. He brushed it aside and said."

"It is not your fault, my son, it is the generation gap."

36

Kashmir Shaivism and the Southern Link

> Kashmir Saivism has penetrated to that depth of living thought where diverse currents of human wisdom unite in a luminous syntheses. — Rabindranath Tagore

THE horses were getting tired, though they were mountain animals used to the hardships of the weather and the gradient. But sage Ramanujam was in two minds whether to return on his own or to carry on. The precious burden on the second horse, which his *shishya* was riding, was the cause of it all. The packhorses following them were trying bravely to keep up. But it was difficult. Suddenly, a shout from his *shishya* brought the sage to a halt. They were being followed and the pursuers were twenty strong and determined to catch up with them. Beckoning to his disciple, the sage said, 'Let us wait for them there is no point in killing the animals'.

Cresting a small hill, they waited the horses grateful for a breather. The sage dismounted and waited for the pursuers to catch up. They came and stopped a little away from them. They were armed. But sage Ramanujam disarmed them by holding out a bundle in his hand and offering it to them. The leader dismounted came, bowed, took the bundle and without a word went back, mounted his horse, gestured to his men and returned to Vitasta from where they had come.

And the sage was sad. From Kancheepuram, he travelled on foot and on horseback to reach Kashyap Rishi's land to look at the holy manuscripts and texts and if possible to carry them with him back to his native land. But it was not to be. All the wisdom contained in those texts would have to remain there and he would have to return empty handed. "Master, why are you looking so sad and despondent." the *shishya* asked his master.

"Because, we have lost all that we came for."

"You mean, the manuscripts and the texts?"

"Yes, of course."

"No master, we have not lost everything. On the contrary, we have gained everything. After all, knowledge is to be shared, it is meant for distribution, and we have it."

"How do you say that?"

"While, we were riding, master, I read the texts and memorised them. It is all there, master. Bhagvan has helped me to remember everything that was in them."

"Vishnu be praised", said the sage.

Legend has it that this was the beginning of the link between the two philosophies of Shaivism and Vaishnava doctrines.

Kashmir Shaivism has its own place of distinction in the theistic Indian thought. "It is a well postulated doctrine that so far as six schools of Indian Philosophy are concerned, despite the apparent diversity in their approach to the tackling of the nature of Ultimate reality, they are in essence in the theistic Indian thought." Says Mr. L.K. Swaroop in his research article in Sarada, Ramakrishna Mission, Srinagar.

That Shaivism did influence the Buddhist philosophy is borne out by its own development especially in the context of Kashmir, since the valley was a part of the Ashokan empire. Mahayana, which may rightly be, called a synthesis of the concept of Shiva and Shakti and of the early Buddhist philosophy attained singular popularity and became a force not only in northern India, but also in Central Asia and China.

By the end of the eighth century AD, Buddhism lost much of its pristine glory and was slowly supplanted by the re-emerging philosophy of India. Buddhism never ousted Hinduism from any large part of

India and the two systems co-existed right from the death of Buddha till about the tenth century AD.

Kashmir Shaivism known as Trika-Shastra or simply Trika is so called either because it accepts as most important the triad: Siddha, Namaka and Malini out of the ninety two *Agamas*, recognised by it, or because the triad consisting of Shiva, Shakti and Anu Kor again of Shiva, Shakti and Nara, or lastly of the Goddesses Para, Apara and Paratpara is recognised or because it explains the three modes of knowledge of Reality, non-dual (*abheda*), nondual-cum-dual (*bhedabeda*) and dual (*bheda*).

Note the many ors in the explanation. Either this or that, or that. The modem man will question that it is not definite, accurate, material and analytical in its interpretation. But what is forgotten is that synthesis was the bedrock of ancient philosophy and science. Today, we have to go to about twenty specialists to find out definitely what is wrong with our body. And even after that it is may, likely, possibly, probably. Ancient systems took the entire entity as one looked at it as one, and interpreted it as one. If there were more than one possibility or explanation, it was presented before the student or the scholar.

Kashmir Shaivism is essentially a spiritual philosophy, because its doctrines regarding; reality, the world and man are derived from a wealth of spiritual experiences. Its greatest exponents were *yogins* of high stature who showed wonderful insight into abstruse points of philosophy. It has beel recognised that various kinds of disciplines, which may be called *yoga*, reveal the science of the inner being and nature of man, as also the art of using the powers of knowledge and action hidden at present in unknown regions of our being and nature.

The Trika or Kashmir Shaivism is a rational exposition of a view of Reality obtained primarily through more than normal experience of Yoga and divine revelation.

Harmony is the watchword of Trika. The Trika, however, does not stop with the deliverance of the soul from *maya*, from the delusion of duality; it goes further to the concept of divination of the soul, which means the recognition of its own identity with Paramashiva.

And this recognition is the same as realising identity with everything and also freedom from everything says the eminent Kashmir historian P.N.K. Bamzai.

Kashmir Shaivism reached its apogee (the highest point of development) in the 12th century AD. Both Kashmir Shaivism and the South Indian Shaivism have close affinities which is apparent from the fact that Kashmir Shaivism and Shaiva Siddhanta build up their doctrine from the basic concept of India from the extreme north to the extreme south from time immemorial. This was possible by the free exchange of books between and visits of saints and savants to Kashmir and south India. Remember, in those days, there were no passports and visas. The artificial barriers which the modern man has built round himself though science and technology has given him what Marshal Mcluhan called the Global Village meaning thereby that the world is one big entity. Radio and television signals beamed through satellites today do not recognise national boundaries, and yet we maintain that we are the jingoistic citizens of this country or that.

Knowledge does not recognise national boundaries and despite the handicaps of communication, transport, printing, etc., knowledge did travel from one end to the other country often on horseback or even the bare back of the seekers of knowledge.

Whether Shankaracharya travelled to Kashmir or not, the temple in his name must certainly have some connection with him. And scholars do say that as a result of his visit, Kashmir Shaivists transformed the older form of dualistic Shaivism as prevailing in Kashmir to that of the basic concept of the Vedanta. But south Indian Shaivism itself traces its origin to Kashmir.

It is known that Thirumular, one of the earliest teachers of Shaivism in the South(he is placed some time between the first and the ninth centuries AD) came from the land of Pratyabhijna School, that is Kashmir. It is also known that the Chola kings of the tenth and eleventh centuries AD imported many Shaiva teachers from the north to come and teach Shaivism to their people. Recently (several decades back) several important manuscripts of works of famous Kashmiri

Shaiva philosophers in Sarada and some south Indian scripts have been found in Kerala and Tamil Nadu.

"How much older Kashmir Shaivism may have been in its origin is not easy to determine" observes Dr. Nilakantha Shastri. There are elements in common between the dogmatic of Kashmir Shaivism and those of south Indian Shaivism.

> Yet in their philosophy, they differ perceptibly, the Kashmir school being idealistic and the south Indian pluralist in metaphysics. The historical relations between the two forms is not easy to decide, though the mention of Brahmans from Kashmir in south Indian inscriptions may lead one to infer that south Indian Shaivism is also ultimately derived from Kashmir. Literary and epigraphic evidence from South India and Java and other Indian colonies of the East also connects the origin and spread of Shaivism with the march of Agastya from the North to the South and his further progress towards the Eastern lands",

Says Professor Shastri in his celebrated work, *The Cultural Heritage of India*.

It may have escaped our present-day scientific temper-minded experts that philosophy and culture do not have check-post and border line to delineate their areas. It may have check-post and border lines to delineate their areas. It may have escaped the attention of many since temples have been with us for thousands of years that their location was also scientific.

If today you start from Madras and traverse the southern peninsula without looking at the map to see whether you are in Tamil Nadu or Andhra or Karnataka or Kerala and mark on a blank map, the Shiva temples found in the area, you will even at first glance see that the figure of 8 have some similarity, equality between its two halves. What that means is for the scholars to unearth and tell us, for it must mean something to have temples located in a uniform or systematic line that does lead to some place and some conclusion.

The duality, rather plurality of our beliefs takes in all. That is why we have survived the longest. And it is the invisible link, which does become visible in times of crisis like the present one. Maybe, this will be apparent to us more clearly, when the time comes. Until then, let us revel in the thought that we are one and shall remain one.

37

Spreading the Buddha's Gospel

The India-China Link

BETWEEN 900 and 1000 years after Buddha's *samadhi*, Buddhism travelled far and wide and between third and eighth century AD. Kashmir was not only a strong centre of learning of Buddhist culture and philosophy, but also geared to the propagation of the faith beyond India's border.

Traditionally, Hinduism has been a religion that did not propagate the faith to those who did not subscribe to it. Unlike the religions, that followed Hinduism, it has been content to seek its own path with full autonomy of method and regularity of worship. In modern parlance, it may be described as inner party democracy. The freedom given within the broad parameters defines the choice, but designates the objective. This freedom has been enjoyed for centuries by a majority of the Hindus and abused by a small minority.

That is perhaps the reason given by Kamala Das while defending her decision to leave the Hindu fold. She cited the reason as 'too much of freedom in Hinduism'. But back in ancient times in Kashmir, Buddhism co-existed with Hinduism since most of the kings adhered to the cardinal principle of no persecution of people professing different faiths.

We have heard of Chinese scholars and travellers like Fa-hein, Hieun-Tsang, coming to India as also people like Al-Beruni and Bernier and leaving valuable writings for posterity. But we have not heard of Indian travellers going to China to propagate the word of the Buddha.

Today (AD 2000), the ignorance about China in India is abysmal.

The whole world knows that India has 35 States and when the plague broke out in Surat and more recently when cyclone hit Orissa, the entire world knew about it because they had read or heard about it. But if one asks a university graduate as to how many provinces there are in China he will not know. Apart from Shanghai and Beijing and recently Hong-Kong and Macau, he will not be able to name a few provinces. Indians find difficulty to pronounce Chinese names. Thus, it becomes all the more astonishing that Kashmirian Buddhist scholars went to China, learnt their language and translated Indian Buddhist religious texts into Chinese.

Our story begins with a Brahman encountering a Buddhist monk. A Kashmiri Brahman, no believer in Buddhism, heard a knock at his door. On opening it, he found a Buddhist Monk who asked for alms. The old Brahman go enraged and attacked him and turned him out. Retribution followed soon. "The hand that had struck the monk was paralysed and in order to expiate the sin, the Brahman went in search of the monk. He requested him to come to his house and meekly and devoutly begged for his pardon and to show his deep reverence to the monk offered him his only son Yasa to be taken into the fold. The monk accepted him. Yasa was then only 13 years of age and after undergoing a thorough training in the various Buddhist texts, was given the robe of a monk.

At the age of 27 he left for China to preach to the people there. He reached Kashgar where while partaking of a feast given annually by the Chief who became his devout follower kept him in Kashgar for a number of years. It was here that he came in contact with Kumarajiva who was travelling to Kucha and who stayed in Kashgar for sometime. Both of them worked together at some translations when the Chinese invaded Kucha. The chief of Kashgar went to its aid leaving Yasa in-charge of his son. But he was too late, Kucha having meanwhile fallen to the Chinese general and Kumarajiva taken as a prisoner to China. When Kumarajiva died, Yasa lost heart and returned to Kashmir. Between AD 410-13 he had translated four works into the Chinese among which were Dirghatama and Dharamaguptaka Vinaya. He was a monk of high moral sense and refused to accept any presents in cash or kind from anybody, saying that 'to accept presents was derogatory to a monk', says renowned scholar P. Dattatreya. a specialist on ancient Kashmir in a chapter entitled "Kashmiri Buddhist Missionaries in China" in Bikhu Chaman Lal's monumental work *India, cradle of cultures*.

"Kashmir", says Dr. P. C. Bagchi, "takes the leading part in the transmission of Buddhist Traditions directly to China. The number of Buddhist scholars who went to China from Kashmir is larger than that of those who went from other parts of India. Kashmir was the most flourishing centre of Buddhist learning in India in this period. It was the centre of the most powerful Buddhist sect of Notthern India, the Sarvastivada."

Perhaps the most famous of the Kashmirian Buddhist missionaries was the celebrated Kumarajiva. He was the son of Kumarayan a native of Kashmir who was the minister of a petty *raja*. He went to Kucha in Central Asia where he rose to the position of Rajguru. Then he fell in love with a Princess named Jeva and married her. Kumarajiva was the offspring of that marriage. But soon after his birth, his mother became a nun and brought him up herself. From Kucha she took her infant son to Kashmir for his education where he studied under a Buddhist scholar Bandhudatta. After completing his studies in Kashmir, Kumarajiva along with large number of Kashmirian scholars returned to Kucha, where he established a monastery and started work in the translation of Buddhist texts in Sanskrit into Chinese.

Very soon, his fame spread and he was recognised as a learned scholar who also had knowledge of Vedas. In AD 383 Fu-Chien, Emperor of the Tsin dynastery conquered Kucha and Kumarajiva along with other Kashmirian scholars were taken prisoner. His chief captor Lu-kuang who was the General in-charge of Kucha wanted to settle there, but his chief prisoner Kumarjiva predicted that his destiny lay elsewhere. So both the captor and the captive went to China where Lu-kuang became the ruler of southern Liang and Kumarajiva his chief advisor. But he also became one of the greatest scholars in Chinese Buddhism. The Chinese Emperor requested him to go to his capital in AD 401, where he carried on his work of propagation, writing and translation till his death in AD 413. Along with two collaborators Yasa and Vimalaksha, he gave a Chinese orientation to the teachings of the Buddha. The most important work produced during this period was Saddarmapundarika, 'Lotus Flower Scripture of the Mysterious Law'.

Apart from a large number of Kashmiri Scholars who contributed to taking the gospel of the Buddha to China, some of them were like Sanghabut, who went to China in AD 381 Gautamasangha who went in AD 384 or Punyatrata who went at the end of the fourth century AD, Charmayasa who went there in AD 397, Buddhayasa, Vimalaksha in AD 406, Buddhajiva went to South China as a companion and collaborator of the famous Chinese traveller and scholar Fa-hein in AD 423.

But one of the greatest sons of Kashmir who was responsible for converting the whole of Java and the neighbouring Islands to the Buddhist faith was Gunaverma. He was a prince of the royal family of Kashmir. His grandfather Haribhadra being a tyrant was banished from his kingdom and had to spend the rest of his life as a wanderer in mountains and marshes. His father, Sanganand, also was an exile, From his very childhood Gunaverma was religious by nature and at an early age he thoroughly grasped the Buddhist Scriptures and committed thousands of *sutras* to memory. It appears that at that time the king of Kashmir died issueless and nobles and ministers decided to invite Gunaverma to be the king. But he was so imbued with the religious missionary zeal that he refused the offer and instead started on a long pilgrimage to the holy Buddhist places in India. He then went to Sri Lanka where he was warmly welcomed by the Buddhist community. He worked with eminent scholars there and was responsible for improving the customs of the people in the community. Then he went to Java.

Fa-hein tells us that in AD 418 Brahmanism flourished in Java and the Buddhist were not worth mentioning. This, however, changed altogether only a few years later due to the preachings of Gunaverma. The king and his family were the first to be converted by him to the Buddhist faith in AD 423. And the population soon followed suit. Being a Kashmiri, Gunaverma was most probably a Sarvastivadin which explains the study of this school of philosophy by the Javanese Buddhists. Gunaverma's fame spread far and wide and emissaries from the neighbouring islands came in large numbers inviting him to visit their homeland.

At last, the Emperor of China also came to know about his work and the Buddhist theologians then requested him to send emissaries to Java to ask Gunaverma to visit China. When they came he decided to go to Nanking where he reached in AD 431. After converting nearly all the islands on the way. In Nanking, the Emperor himself went out to receive him and built a magnificent monastery. Gunaverma was, however, destined to live only for a year in Nanking where he died in AD 432. But this last year of his life was of intense activity since no less than fourteen works were either translated or written by him during this period.

The mention of Jetavan monastery leads to another Kashmirian monk who was there and probably met Gunaverma in AD 431. He was Dharmamitra a famous teacher of Shyana or meditative school. He translated several Sanskrit works on meditation into the Chinese language and also taught a large number of students this branch of Buddhist philosophy. He was a quiet worker. At first he had gone to Kucha where the authorities would not allow him to proceed to China. He, however, evaded the frontier guards and reached Tu-huang where he founded a monastery and planted thousands of trees round it. It was in AD 424 that when he went to South China and lived there till his death in AD 442. He translated twelve Buddhists texts into the Chinese language.

Buddhaverman, another Kashmiri monk, went to Western China shortly before AD 433 and being a specialist in Vibhasa, translated *Mahavibhasa Shastra* in 160 chapters during AD 437-9. Ratnacinta who originally belonged to a royal Kashmiri family and was a specialist in Vinaya. He went to China reaching O-yang in AD 693 and founded a monastery there named Tien-chu-sse, 'The monastery of India' and translated seven works from Sanskrit between AD 693 to 706. He died in AD 721.

During the tenth century AD the Chinese annals mention the

name of Tien-si-taai, native of Kashmir who came to the Chinese capital and was put in charge of board of translators by the Chinese Emperor and it was as a result of his efforts that the board was able to enrich the Chinese Buddhist literature by more than two hundred works. In 1005 another Kashmiri monk, Mu-lo-she-ki went to China and carried on the missionary work in collaboration with many more Indian monks.

Note: The above is the result of almost a lifetime spent on research by Revered Bhiku Chaman Lal (*India, Cradle of Cultures*, 1976).

Bibliography

Cunningham, A., Coins of Medieval India, 1894.

Atreyi, Biswas, The political History of the Hunas in India, 1973 Bilhana, Vikramankadevacarita.

Cunningham, A., Ancient Geography of India, 1871.

Kak, R.C., Handbook of the Archaeological and Numismatic Society of the S.P.S. Museum, 1923.

Pandey, D.B., The Sahis of Afghanistan and Punjab, 1973 Sarkar,

D.C., Studies in the Society and Administration of Ancient and Medieval India, 1967.

Havell, E.B., Aryan Rule in India.

Goetz, Hermann, Studies in the History and Art of Kashmir and The India Himalayas, 1969.

Wilson, H.H., The Hindu History of Kashmir, 1960.

Chatterji, J.C., Kashmir Saivism, 1962.

Kilam, Jia Lal, A History of Kashmiri Pandits, 1955.

Ferguson, J. P., Kashmir - A Historical Introduction, 1996.

Stein, M.A., Introduction to Kalhana's Rajatarangini, 1961.

Bazaz, P. N., Daughters of the Vitasta, 1959.

Gervis, Pearce, This is Kashmir, 1954.

Bamzai, P. N. K., A History of Kashmir, 1973.

Kalhana, Rajatarangini, translated by M.A. stein, 1961.

Khosla, Sarla, Buddhism in Kashmir, 1972.

Pandit, R.S., Kalhana's Rajatarangini, translated in 1968.

Smith, V.A., The Early History of India, 1957.

Lawrence, W.R., The Valley of Kashmir, 1895.

Chaman Lal, India, Cradle of Cultures, 1976.

Index